Music Experiences for Young Children

Michele Wilt

Michele Wilt, a graduate of the Dalcroze School of Music in New York City, has taught music to children both privately and in various music schools for more than fifteen years. She has also conducted workshops at the Eastman School of Music of the University of Rochester, Ithaca College, Concordia College, the Botsford School of the Dance, and various MENC chapters.

Her music experience includes study at the Institute of Musical Art, and with Carlos Buhler. She has played in concert performances in ensemble for the National Music League and the WQXR Artist Series.

Mrs. Wilt is coauthor of the "Music Discovery Activity Cards" (The Center for Applied Research in Education, 1978), another practical music education aid for music specialists and classroom teachers. The series includes six sets of individualized activities exploring six basic areas of music.

Mrs. Wilt presently teaches music at the Dalcroze School of Music.

The Center for Applied Research in Education, Inc.
West Nyack, New York 10994

Library of Congress Cataloging in Publication Data

Wilt, Michele.
  Music experiences for young children.

  Lessons ; songs with piano acc. and story
time activities.
  1. School song-books. 2. Singing games.
I. Title.
M1993.W776   372.8'7   81-38513
ISBN 0-87628-588-4   AACR2

About Music Experiences
for Young Children

This is a book for all teachers of young children. It seeks to provide a store of experiences that will foster a love for music as a fundamental and happy part of living.

Included are over thirty-five detailed lessons in which children can participate wholly, to engage their imaginations, their feeling for movement, their attention, and their musical sensitivities. The lesson material is uniquely adapted to develop the child's ability to listen, to sense his or her own bodily rhythms, and to respond to the beat, its divisions, and variations of tempo and dynamics. It will encourage the child to sing freely and to develop an awareness of pitch and tone. It provides a framework for improvisation in song, in movement, or on an instrument. It makes use of well-chosen music and songs related to the child's world.

Every effort has been made to present these music experiences in a form accessible not only to the music specialist, but to the classroom teacher, the kindergarten teacher, the teacher of Head Start and Day Care programs, and any other individual involved in early childhood education.

The Content of the Lessons

Each lesson in this book provides as much material as possible for a whole experience. Each has its own imaginative impetus, a song, activities involving movement, an opportunity to use the material in some improvisatory manner, and a story related to the content of the lesson to be acted out in song and movement. In most lessons, the beginning of notation is also included.

Each activity is introduced as it might be in a classroom, addressed directly to the children, with dialogue in bold type. This is not meant to be used literally, but it is an effort to suggest an atmosphere that might be useful to the teacher. Specific directions for carrying out the activities are printed in regular type.

Much of the material is based on familiar folk songs, chants, and traditional rhymes. The rhythms are natural ones—walking, running, skipping, galloping, and swinging. The activities stem from the everyday life and environment of the child and from stories of the imagination.

Many of the lessons develop one aspect of a musical subject. For example, "I Go UP and I Go DOWN" deals with the rise and fall of pitch, "Hurry Up!" presents changes of tempo, and "Merry October" is about note values. Some lessons are concerned with the natural world of the child and his or her participation in it—the flight of birds, the elephant in the zoo, sailing on the ocean, being a cloud. Others are holiday lessons, for Thanksgiving, Christmas, and Halloween. A list of musical subjects touched upon in the lessons is provided on page 13.

The songs, appropriately short for the young child, are fun to sing and easy to learn. The stories that conclude each lesson are based on the materials of the lesson. Individual parts, to be acted out in song and movement, can be taken by one child or many children.

Structure of the Lessons

Each lesson is structured as a complete unit, suitable for use with either small or large groups. Length can vary from 25 to 60 minutes, depending on the age of the children and the time available. However, the material is extremely flexible. It is possible to spend more or less time on different lesson activities, to carry over part of a past lesson, or perhaps to use the material in relation to a classroom event. At different times, either the song or the story may be used alone or to initiate following activities.

Many of the lesson activities can be repeated many times successfully, providing for variation in execution or growing skill in the child's response. For example, the jack-in-the-box activity in Lesson 2, which calls for a quick response in going up and down, is fun to do out of its context in the lesson.

The Music for the Lessons

Although written with a piano accompaniment, the songs can be played with the melodic line alone, on the piano or any other pitched instrument. The activities are carried out, as noted in the lessons, with the aid of a drum or a pitched instrument, which could be a piano, xylophone, or bells.

Sources for recorded music are given for all lesson activities where more sound is desirable. All of the records are drawn from "The RCA Basic Record Library for Elementary Schools," listed on page 9.

Special piano arrangements for all of the recorded music provide an alternative to the records. The arrangements, on pages 197-217, are referred to by a number which follows the record citation in the lesson. Basic considerations in creating the arrangements were rhythmic clarity and ease of performance.

A Song Book for Each Child

The song for each lesson, with its illustration, is printed on a separate page and can be duplicated. Assembled within looseleaf covers, these song pages will make a complete song book for each child. Apart from the pleasure in having one's own music book, such a book provides an excellent first association of sound with the musical symbols.

**

Successful use of *Music Experiences for Young Children* is not dependent on the special skills of the teacher. It was written with confidence that the lessons will make possible the active participation of both the teacher and the child, in an atmosphere of spontaneity, humor, and shared love for musical activity.

Michele Wilt

Contents

CONTENTS

Bringing Music to Your Pupils

If you have the right point of view, the right approach to bringing music to your children, then many seeming impossibilities are at once and amazingly transformed into possibilities.

> *Dr. James L. Mursell*
> *Music and the Classroom Teacher**

To sing and move in rhythm are deep-rooted impulses common to all people. When you participate with children in a music experience, you are drawing on a heritage that belongs to you and can find meaningful expression as much in the world of the child as in a more sophisticated medium.

The following information and suggestions will help you and your pupils use the music experiences in this book to best advantage. Included are a list of materials used in the lessons, suggestions for use of the lessons, and a list of musical subjects that are touched upon in the lessons.

Materials Used in the Lessons

The materials needed for presenting these music experiences are simple and already available in the typical elementary school. They include:

Room with adequate space for movement

Piano and/or record player

NOTE: *Records in the lessons are taken from "The RCA Basic Record Library for Elementary Schools," Vol. I WE-71, Vol. II WE-72, Vol. III WE-73, and WE-87 ("Singing Games"). They can be obtained from any educational record supplier.*

Resonator bells
Xylophone
Drums (big and small)
Rhythm sticks
Triangles
Wood blocks

---

*New York: Silver Burdett Co., 1951, p. 71. This book is valuable reading for any teacher.

Wrist bells
Temple blocks
Tambourines
Rattles
Cymbal
Finger cymbals
Claves
Chalkboard
Note cards (about 7″ square):
Looseleaf cover for each child

A xylophone or other pitched instrument can be substituted for the piano in all lessons.

Suggestions for Use of the Lessons

Room

A good room arrangement is a space adequate for the group to move, with a half-circle of chairs and the piano at one side. This allows for an easy transition from an activity involving movement to one in which everyone is seated. However, since classrooms vary in size and number of children, reasonable alternatives chosen by you are most desirable. For example, in a small space with many children it would be better to do the same skipping exercise twice, with two sets of children. One set might clap while the other children skip.

If possible, let the children go barefoot. It makes a considerable difference in their bodily sensitivity and in their freedom to move. It also makes the experience a little out of the ordinary.

General Attitude

In general, cumulative learning experiences are better than much specific correction. For example, many of the lessons involve such activities as matching tones and echo songs, which will lead in time to better pitch awareness. The same applies to rhythmic activities. Accuracy of response is not the first consideration. Encourage the children to use their bodies freely and expressively. Imaginative involvement, such as "being a tiger," is the best stimulus. The activities provide opportunity for a varied use of the body and for relationships of time and energy, which will result in more sensitive and accurate movement.

Some of the lessons suggest that the children should run "on your toes." In all accuracy, this should be "on the balls of your feet," but the latter seems to be less well understood than "on your toes." This applies to steps faster than the walk. Encourage the heel-to-toe movement in walking to develop a good sense of balance and ease of movement.

Teaching the Songs

The songs, appropriate in length and difficulty for young children, can for the most part be learned in the lesson time. Often, activities will become a part of the song, as in Lesson 11 where the cobbler sings the song as he mends shoes (tapping on a wood block).

For the predominantly two-phrase song, use these guidelines:

- Sing the song without accompaniment. If desired, play the single melodic line on a pitched instrument as you sing.
- Discuss the words, making sure that all are understood. For example, explain the meaning of "dell" in "The Farmer in the Dell."
- Sing the first phrase again and then have the children sing the first phrase with you.
- Sing the second phrase again and then have the children sing the second phrase with you.
- Sing the whole song with the children.
- Sing the whole song with the children as you play the accompaniment.

Repetition of the songs is invaluable. Apart from the pleasure in having a repertoire of songs, the training of the memory is an important factor in musical learning. Often, the singing of several songs with movement can enliven a part of the classroom day apart from the music period.

Give every child as many opportunities as possible to sing alone, with encouragement and approval regardless of skill. Finding the song to sing in his or her music book is a good beginning in associating sound with its written symbols.

Value of Improvisation

The efforts involved in improvisation—in movement, song, or with instruments—are invaluable. Even the smallest achievement has an influence on musical understanding. It is the beginning of an insight into all of music-making.

Notes on Stories

The stories can also become the impetus for the lessons. They often succeed through repetition, perhaps with the children taking different parts. Although the drum is notated for the activities in the story, it is certainly possible to use the music, either recorded or played on the piano, which has been part of the lesson for corresponding activities.

Relaxation

A relaxed body is the basis from which all good movement starts and to which it returns. It provides for the best use of energy, which is often misused because of wrong tension or undue slackness. Children, as well as adults, first must learn to recognize the feeling of the relaxed state and then develop the ability to return to it. There is a constant interchange between the use of energy and relaxation.

In every lesson, try to find the time for a short period of relaxation. This can come between any two activities. Have the children sink slowly to the floor and close their eyes. Encourage them to think of themselves as lying on the summer grass or on a soft bed. They might be rag dolls or sleepy cats. Use any image that will foster "letting go."

Test different arms and legs to see if they are really "soft" like those of a rag doll. At different times, you can play a short quiet piece, such as Record 41-6096 S6B1 or the piano piece from Lesson 25, or hum a simple melody. A period of silence also has its own value in encouraging a state of relaxation without an outside influence.

Two or three minutes on the floor are usually sufficient, after which the children can rise slowly and stretch, and the lesson is resumed.

Order of the Lessons

Please note that the lessons are not sequential in difficulty, although the early lessons are geared for the very youngest children. These early lessons can be used for older children with slight changes in presentation. Also note that in the very youngest group, some children may not participate outwardly for many weeks. They can still be very observant, however, and become excellent participants when they are "ready." In the beginning lessons for the very youngest children, the song pictures and story element in the lessons are a good focus for attention.

Comment on Preparation

You will find it very helpful to go through the lesson before class time, memorize the song, play the music for the different activities, and become familiar with the story. (The children's natural beat will be a bit faster than yours.) This preparation will give you a most advantageous ease, and allow you to use the material with spontaneity and freedom.

Musical Subjects

Musical subjects that are touched upon in the various lessons include:

Rhythm:	the beat and its divisions; groupings of beats (measure); rhythmic pattern; rests; regular and irregular rhythms; accompaniment patterns; conducting; agogic and dynamic accent; the aleatoric experience.
Pitch:	feeling for tonality; high and low; going up and down; repeated tones (recognition); matching tones (in singing); scale by number; recognition and repetition of small melodic phrases; major, minor, and pentatonic modes; response to one or more voices; cadence recognition.
Form:	the musical theme; question and answer; A B A; solo and accompaniment; antiphonal and solo-response phrases; solo and chorus; phrasing; instrument ensemble; design.
Dynamics/Performance Style:	loud and soft; crescendo and decrescendo; tone; staccato and legato; expressive possibilities.
Texture:	smooth, rough, lumpy; soft and hard; stiff and limp.
In Movement:	awareness of self; use of the body; orientation to space; tension and relaxation; coordination; sense of balance; plasticity; rhythms of life; nature; the imagination.
Improvisation:	in song, movement, at the piano or xylophone, or with percussion instruments.
Use of Instruments:	recognition; response to timbre; pitch; descriptive qualities.
Beginnings of Notation:	(in lessons for older children).

The lessons in this book will be an introduction to many forms of music. With your encouragement, they will provide the basis upon which the child can draw the great expressive and illuminating forces of music into his or her everyday world.

The Yellow Bird

Brightly

Good morn - ing, good morn - ing, good morn - ing lit - tle

Yel - low Bird,

(teacher speaking) and little Yellow Bird answers:

Good morn-ing to you.

Lesson 1
THE YELLOW BIRD

1   The children are seated. Have everyone look at the picture of Yellow Bird on the song page.

Yellow Bird really likes it when we sing "Good Morning" to her. She answers, too. Listen—

Sing the song, without accompaniment. (If you wish, play the melodic line on a piano or a pitched instrument as you sing.)

And little Yellow Bird answers—

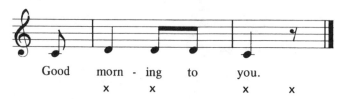

(Later, the children will sing without your speaking.)

2   **Let's all sing to Yellow Bird. We can clap, too. Like this—**

Sing the first part of the song, "Good morning, good morning little Yellow Bird," while clapping. (Claps are marked *x* in the song.)

Now, have the children sing and clap with you. Encourage the clapping only as a physical accompaniment to the singing, with no emphasis on rhythmic accuracy.

That was very good. Let's do it again.

Repeat, perhaps more than once. Continue as suggested in "Teaching the Songs" on page 11.

Sing and clap Yellow Bird's answer, "Good morning to you," and then have the children sing and clap the same.

Repeat this part more than once also.

This time, we'll sing and clap the whole song while I play.

Sing and play with accompaniment, while the children sing and clap the whole song.

And little Yellow Bird answers—

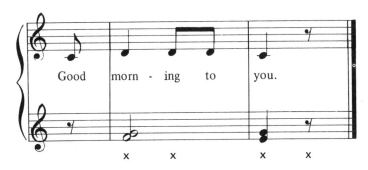

(Later, the children will sing without your speaking.)

That was fine. We'll sing "Good morning" to Yellow Bird tomorrow, too.

3   **Yellow Bird has a swing in her cage. Every day she swings like this—**

(Show.) Standing, swing from side to side, speaking as you move:

Have the children start the swing in their own rhythm. Then add the music.
Play record 41-6091 S3B2 (Piano No. 21).

4   **Sometimes Yellow Bird flies with her friends in the park. We can almost feel like the birds flying if we run on our toes and put out our arms for wings.**

In the beginning, have one or two children "fly" alone, without music. You might "fly" with them.
Give all the children a turn to "fly" in small groups. Then play the music as the children "fly" again, either all together or in small groups.
Play Record 41-6092 S5B3 (Piano No. 17).

5   All the children are seated.

This is a good way to tell us who you are. If you hear me sing your name, sing it back to me.

Sing, with the piano or bells if you wish, to each child. You can also play with the reply.

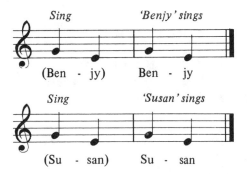

6   **Sometimes Mother Bird calls the baby birds to lunch like this—**

Sing, with the piano or a pitched instrument if you wish:

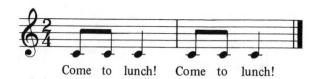

Come to lunch! Come to lunch!

You can hear the sound of her call stay in one place. Let's all sing it.

Sing Mother Bird's call with the children several times.

7   The baby birds have to be sure they know Mother's call. Is this it?

Play in the high register of the piano or a pitched instrument:

Is this it?

Play in the low register of the piano or a pitched instrument:

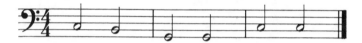

Is this it?

Play the Mother Bird call:

Come to lunch! Come to lunch!

Alternate the above for recognition by the children.

8   Mother Bird's call is in one of my favorite stories. Listen ...

Story Time

Read the story aloud. Then read it aloud again as the individual parts are carried out in movement and song by the children. One or any number of children can take an individual part.

Characters:
Yellow Bird
Baby birds
Singers

Yellow Bird and her children were in the forest. All the baby birds were flying around, but Yellow Bird was seated on the ground in the center. She was busily digging up worms for lunch.

(Yellow Bird is seated, digging worms. Baby birds are flying around.)

Play the drum as Baby birds fly around:

When Yellow Bird had enough for everyone, she called out:

Play on the piano or a pitched instrument as Yellow Bird sings.

Come to lunch! Come to lunch!

The baby birds heard Yellow Bird call. They came and sat beside her. Yellow Bird gave each one a share. They were very hungry and they ate everything up.

(The baby birds sit down beside Yellow Bird. Yellow Bird gives each baby bird a share. All eat.)

Now they sat resting quietly. We sang to Yellow Bird:

Play the piano or a pitched instrument as Singers sing.

Good morn - ing, good morn - ing, good morn - ing lit - tle Yel - low Bird,

Speak. (Later, the children will sing without your speaking.)

And little Yellow Bird answered:

Good morn - ing to you.

Then it was time for Yellow Bird and her children to go, and we watched them fly away. Perhaps we would see them again tomorrow.

(All the birds fly away.)

Play the drum:

𝅘𝅥𝅮𝅘𝅥𝅮 𝅘𝅥𝅮𝅘𝅥𝅮 𝅘𝅥𝅮𝅘𝅥𝅮 𝅘𝅥𝅮𝅘𝅥𝅮 *etc.*

The End

Lesson 2

I Go UP and I Go DOWN

Moderato

I'm go - ing up, I'm go - ing up, And at the top I

think I'll stop, 8 7 6 5 4 3 2 1.

Lesson 2
I GO UP AND I GO DOWN

1   **This morning, as I was passing a toy store, I saw a Jack-in-the-box. "That looks like fun," I thought. Let's all be a Jack-in-the-box.**

    First, listen to the music that makes Jack jump out of the box.

> On a piano, brush up on the keys very fast. (This is best done with the back of the hand held firmly.) On another pitched instrument, play up as fast as possible.

    And here's the music that puts Jack back in the box.

> On a piano, brush down on the keys very fast. (This can be done as above, with the back of the hand held firmly.) On another pitched instrument, play down as fast as possible.
>
> Repeat several times. Say "Up" and "Down" as you play and the children listen.

2   **Now we're in the box. Remember to wait till the music lets you out or puts you back.**

> Have the children kneel and curl over, "in the box."
> They wait, listening, and then spring *up* as you play going *up*.
> They stand and wait, listening, and then they spring *down* as you play going *down*.
> Wait for different time lengths between playing *up* and *down*. That will provide a quick response experience.

3   **Can we take Jack out *very* slowly? Then we'll put him back in the same way.**

> Have the children move with the music as in activity 2 above. This time, play very slowly going up, wait, then play very slowly coming down.

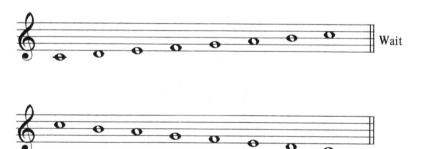

4   The children are seated.

    Jack-in-the-box has his own song. It goes up and down just like Jack. Listen—

Sing the song and teach it to the children.

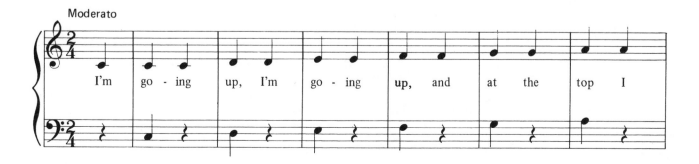

22

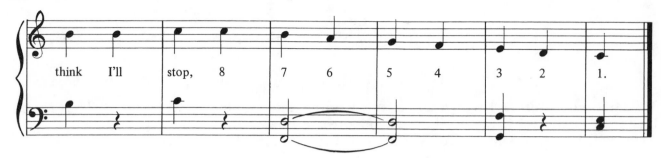

For younger children, sing "la" instead of numbers.

5   Now, when we sing it, make one arm go up and down, too.

Sing with the children. Raise and lower one arm as the song goes up and down.

6

Do the song in different ways, for example:

- Singing with "la" instead of words, in a moderate tempo
- Up and down very fast, with "la."
- Up and down very slowly, with "la."
- Up slowly, singing words, and down fast, with "la," etc.

You might have fun singing Jack's song when you're at home, too. We'll sing it again tomorrow.

7

Put a large drawing on the chalkboard, like this:

Which way is Jack going?

Play either going up or going down on the piano or another pitched instrument, as in Activity 3 above.

Give individual children a turn to go to the board and, after saying which way Jack went, add their own line to the line which shows going up or going down.

8

You will need a xylophone and a stick.

Show how the large end makes low sounds and the small end makes high sounds.

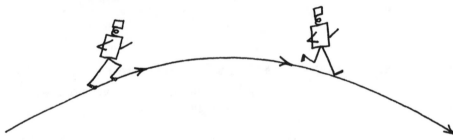

(Show) Speaking-Ex. "I'm going up the hill." Play any tones going up, as you say, "Up, up, up."

Give individual children a turn to say where they are going up, and then to play *up, up, up* on the xylophone, going from low to high.

Any response that indicates going up is good—in an elevator, up into the sky in a balloon, or just "up, up, up" on the xylophone.

9   Now I'm going down.

> (Show) Speaking-Ex. "I'm going down the hill." Play any tones going down, as you say, "down, down, down."
>
> Give individual children a turn to say where they are going down, and then to play *down, down, down* on the xylophone.
>
> Any response that indicates going down is good—sliding down a hill, down in an elevator, down an escalator, or just "Down, down, down" on the xylophone.

10   Your swing in the park goes down—up. Let's say "Down—Up" as we swing our arms in the same way.

> Swing your arms with the children a few times as you all say "Down—Up." Encourage the movement of arms going down with "Down," but do not insist.
>
> Then play as they sing.
>
> Play Record 41-6153 S7B2 (Piano No. 36).

Story Time

Characters
The Sun
Flower Seeds
Singers

Read the story aloud. Then read it aloud again as individual parts are carried out in movement and song by the children. One or any number of children can take an individual part.

(As the story begins, the Sun is curled up on the floor. The Flower Seeds are also curled up on another part of the floor.)

"Time to get up," said the Sun. He knew the Flower Seeds were waiting for him.

Up, up, up he came slowly, until he was high overhead.

Play on the piano or a pitched instrument:

(The Sun comes up slowly.)

He walked to the place where the Flower Seeds were planted in the ground.

Play on the drum:

(The Sun walks.)

When the Flower Seeds felt the warmth of the Sun, they grew tall and strong.

Play on the piano or a pitched instrument:

(The Flower Seeds come up slowly.)

Then the Sun said, "Now I can go home," and he continued on his way.

Play on the drum:

(The Sun walks.)

Soon it was time for him to go down, and we could see him no more.

Play on the piano or a pitched instrument as the Sun goes down slowly:

(The Sun goes down slowly.)

Then everyone was glad to sing the song that went up and down, like the Sun.

Play on the piano or a
pitched instrument as all
sing:

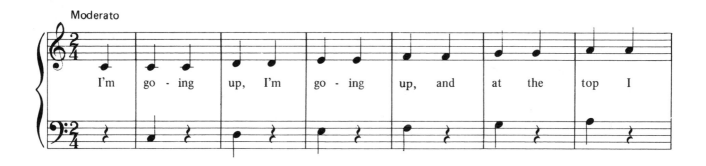

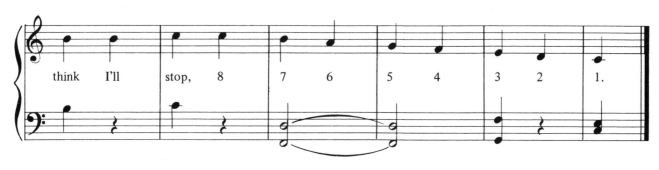

For younger children,
sing "la" instead of
numbers.

The End

Lesson 3

High, So High

Allegro

Come with me, the rob - in said. So

high, so high we'll fly through the sky.

Lesson 3
HIGH, SO HIGH

1   This piano (or xylophone) is just full of all kinds of voices that live inside. Listen. This low note has a voice like the drum.

Play on the piano:

tum   tum   tum

Play on the drum:

Give individual children a turn to play "Tum, tum, tum" on the low note on the piano, and then to play "Tum, tum, tum" on the drum. Give them as much help as necessary.

2   Here's a high note that sings "Ding, ding, ding" like a triangle.

Play on the piano:

ding   ding   ding

Play on the triangle:

Give individual children a turn to play "Ding, ding, ding" on the high note on the piano, and then to play "Ding, ding, ding" on the triangle. Give them as much help as necessary.

3   Let's close our eyes and play a listening game. If I play the drum voice on the piano—the low voice—call out "Tum, tum, tum."

If I play the triangle voice on the piano—the high voice—call out "Ding, ding, ding."

Play low or high as in activities 1 and 2 above. Alternate A B, A B, A A, B B, and so on, between the voices.

4

Have all the children look at the picture of the giraffe on the song page. Make a special observation of his tall neck.

I'll play music with a high voice, while you walk like a giraffe. If you raise your arms and stand up on your toes, you might reach almost as high as he does. Like this—

Do a few steps like a giraffe.

If you hear a low sound, the giraffe is sitting down for a rest.

Play on the piano or a pitched instrument as the children walk like giraffes and sit on the floor as you play the low note.

5 **You looked like very good giraffes.**

The sky is up very high, too. In the daytime we can see the sun there. What else can we see in the sky?

Possible responses: birds, airplanes, clouds, rainclouds, kites, a balloon.

Have one child be the sun, standing still, while everyone else is a cloud floating in the sky. Encourage them to move on their toes, lightly and smoothly.

While moving as clouds, have the children listen for the end when the music goes down, and everyone, including the sun, goes slowly down to the floor.

Have one child play the triangle with you, if you wish, as you play on the piano or a pitched instrument while the children move.

Slowly

6 **Listen to what this robin would like you to do with him—**

Sing the song and teach it to the children.

7

Give two children triangles and give one child a drum.

Let's play our song with instruments. When I play the song very high, the triangles can play with me. When I play the song very low, the drum will play.

Give individual children a turn to play the triangles and drum with you as you play the song in either the high or low register. Recognition of the high and low registers is sufficient. Do not ask for a rhythmic pattern.

8 **Now we can all sing and play together.**

Have the children sing as the triangles and drum play.

Play the piano or a pitched instrument as for activity 6 above. Encourage the instruments to play softly, more as an indeterminate accompaniment than as a rhythmic pattern.

9 **The robin must be waiting for us. Now we can fly with him. When the music stops, come and sit down by the piano.**

Play Record 41-6094 S1B2 (Piano No. 33).

Story Time

Read the story aloud. Then read it aloud again as the individual parts are carried out in movement and song by the children. One or any number of children can take an individual part.

Characters
Two triangles
A Drum
Singers

Once upon a time, two Triangles and a Drum sat quietly in their places, waiting for the Singers to come.

One of the Triangles spoke up: "Don't you think I have a very beautiful high voice?" She played a little song.

 *(Triangle plays.)*

The other Triangle said, "Oh, yes. And I also have a very beautiful high voice." She played a little song, too.

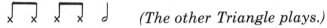 *(The other Triangle plays.)*

"That is so." It was the Drum speaking. "But what can compare with my deep, low sound?" He played:

♩ ♩ ♩ ♩ *(Drum plays.)*

"Can you make such a good low sound?"

One Triangle tried. Her stick played on one side, then on another side, and played stronger and stronger, but no sound was low.

♩ ♩ ♩ ♩ *(Triangle plays.)*

"Perhaps I cannot make a low sound," admitted the Triangle, "but can *you* make a high sound?"

Now the Drum tapped his stick lightly and strongly, at the side and in the center, but he could not make a high sound.

♩ ♩ ♩ ♩ ♩ ♩ ♩ *(Drum plays.)*

Just then the Singers came in. All was quiet for a moment. Then the Triangles and the Drum played the robin's song with the Singers. It sounded very beautiful, and all of them were pleased and happy to do what they could do best.

Play the piano or another pitched instrument as all sing, the triangle plays, and the drum plays:

Come with me the rob-in said. So high, so high we'll fly through the sky.

The End

High Stepping Horses

Briskly

High - step - ping hors - es, All   in   a   ring, Go

step - ping,   step - ping   as   they   sing.

Lesson 4
HIGH-STEPPING HORSES

1   Give the children wrist bells.

Let's go riding on our ponies. I think they would like to run this morning. (Benjy), will you show us how your pony goes running?

> Give other children a turn to show the pony running. Then all can go, as you play the music. If possible, use the word "trot" for the pony's run.
> Play Record 41-6088 S6B3 (Piano No. 3).

2   **Some horses like to step high, like the horses in the circus. They have a special song. Listen—**

> Sing the song and teach it to the children.

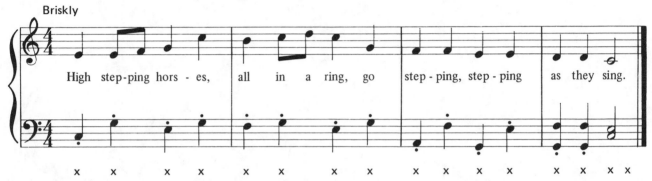

3   **We need a drum to play with our song.**

> Give the children turns to play the drum as they all sing the song and you play the piano or a pitched instrument.
> Encourage a drum beat on the beat marked *x* in the song.

4   **We can teach our horses how to go in a circle as they step high.**

> Use two or four chairs spaced apart to define a circle.

> Take one child with you as you sing the song and step in a circle. Then the other children can step in a circle while singing.
> Now, have all the children go together as they sing and you play as for activity 2 above.

5   **Sometimes the horses stop to eat the grass. When the music stops, let them "eat" until the music starts again.**

> Play again as the children step, but stop at different parts of the song and wait as the horses "eat." Then resume playing.

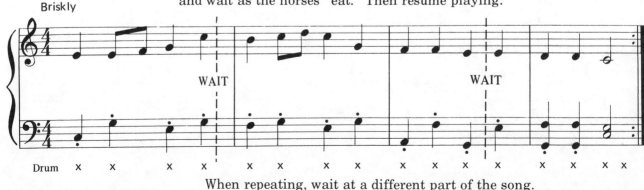

When repeating, wait at a different part of the song.

6   Good. Now I think our horses need shoes.

A big horse has big shoes. We'll have to hammer pretty strongly. Raise your hammer high, like this—

Have the children kneel on the floor.

Show hammering on the floor with a high, strong motion (with the fist of one hand).

Have the children "hammer" shoes with the music.
Play Record 41-6150 S1B1 (Piano No. 37).

7   A small horse has small shoes. We'd better hammer lightly. Keep your hammer close to the floor, like this—

Show hammering on the floor with a low, light motion (with the fist of one hand).

Have the children "hammer" shoes as you play the drum. Play the drum in the same tempo as for hammering big shoes, but very softly.

8   Some horses grow up to be rocking horses. As they rock back and forth they have favorite words.

Show the children how they can stand with one foot forward to rock back and forth as they say:

(Forward)	(Back)
Ride a cock-	horse to
Banbury	Cross to
see a fair	lady ride
on a white	horse.

The verse can be done as a chant, between two notes, as G-E, or E-C.

Ride   a   cock horse   to   Ban - bur - y   Cross

Ride   a   cock horse   to   Ban - bur - y   Cross

A later lesson can go on with

(Forward)	(Back)
Rings on her	fingers and
Bells on her	toes,
She shall have	music where-
ever she	goes.

9   That was fine. Be sure to be a rocking horse again some time today. Now we will have a story about how one horse joined the circus.

Story Time

Read the story aloud. Then read it aloud again as the individual parts are carried out in movement and song by the children. One or any number of children can take an individual part.

Characters
The Brown Horse
Circus Horses
Friend (drummer)

Once upon a time there was a beautiful Brown Horse. One day he went to the circus.

He saw the circus horses dressed in sparkling costumes. They were stepping high in a perfect circle, as they sang:

(Circus horses step high and sing.)

Played on the piano or
a pitched instrument:

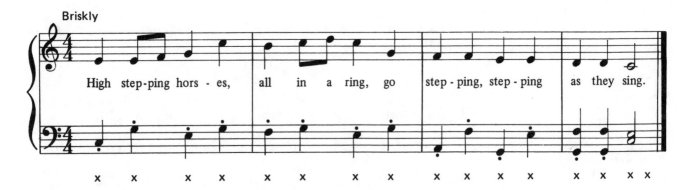

"Oh," he thought, "I would like to be in the circus, too." So he asked his friend to play the drum while he learned to step high with the music and to go in a circle.

Play as above.

(The Brown Horse steps high in a circle.
His friend plays the drum, marked x.)

Now he could join the circus! He was the happiest horse in the world.

The next day we saw him with all the other horses as they sang and stepped high.

Play as above.

(All step high in a circle and sing.)

The End

Lesson 5

Toot! Toot!

Allegro

Toot! Toot! Toot! Toot! Chug, chug, chug, chug, chug, chug, chug, it's

com - ing down the track. Toot! Toot! Toot!___

Lesson 5
TOOT! TOOT!

1

The children are seated.
Draw one or more figures like this on the chalkboard.

Who will color the toes?
Good. Later, we'll draw some toes in our drawing books.
Now everyone take hold of *your* toes.

Have one or two children color in the toes. Call for answers to questions like these:

Did we go up or down to find our toes?
Are they "high" or "low?"

2 **What do you think your toes see when you go barefoot in the park?**

Possible responses: grass, the sandbox, people's shoes, dogs, cats, worms.

You can be the worms going for a trip around the park fence. I'll play music with a low voice, too.

(Two chairs at opposite ends of a space will define a fence.)
Play on the piano or another pitched instrument as the children crawl on the floor around the "fence" in free movement.

Very slowly, not in strict time

3 **Those were really good worms. Now, maybe your toes are in the sandbox.**

Encourage the children to move their feet freely, their toes grasping and digging in the sand.

4 **Now we come into the house. Maybe our toes see the cat. He's looking for a mouse, so he goes *very* slowly.**

Play the drum slowly, or play the piano or another pitched instrument as in this example, while the children move like cats.

Slowly

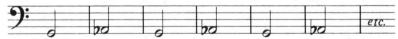

5 **Who is this?**

Play on the drum, very fast and lightly in short spurts, until the children recognize the mice.

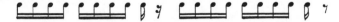

Play again as the children move like mice. Play either the drum or the piano or another pitched instrument, as in this example:

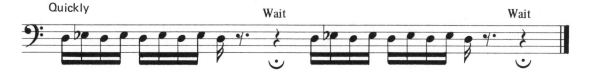

6 Now if we all listen very carefully to the low voice of the music, it will tell us what is happening.

When the mice hear the cat moving, they run and hide.

When the cat is still, the mice come out and run around.

> Have one child be the cat while the rest of the children are mice.
>
> Alternate playing the cat and mouse music with short periods of silence (cat—wait—mice—cat—wait—etc.).
>
> The mice can "hide" very still on the floor when the cat music plays, or they can hide under chairs, or a desk. The cat can stay very still on the floor when the music for the mice is played.

7

> The children are seated.

That was fun. We'll do it again some time.

When we were outside, we might have heard a bird singing like this—

> Play on the piano or the xylophone and sing:

Chirp chirp, Chirp chirp

> Give individual children a turn to play the high note as everyone sings "Chirp, chirp." (Show the child the high part of the piano or the xylophone and help with the playing if necessary.)

8 Then, from far off, we might have heard the whistle of a train. "Toot! Toot!" it calls.

> Play on the piano or xylophone and sing:

Toot!   Toot!

> Give individual children a turn to play the relatively lower tone of middle C for "Toot! Toot!" as everyone sings (middle C—the note in front of two black notes in the center of the piano).

C 🎹

> For younger children, cover both sides of the piano keyboard with cardboard, leaving the middle octave open from G to G.

9 We have a song about "Toot Toot!" and the train.

> Sing the song and teach it to the children.

com - ing down the track. Toot! Toot! Toot!___

10 The train is moving. Let's clap while we say "Chug chug" for the sound the engine makes.

Clap with the children.

Use your voice to guide the clapping from very slow to very fast, in a gradual speeding up. Then return to very slow, in a gradual slowing down. Stop the train with "T-o-o-t! T-o-o-t! T-o-o-t! T-o-o-t!"

11 Now we can take our train on a ride. Remember to start very slowly. When you hear "Toot! Toot!" it means the train is coming to a station and is slowing down to stop.

Have the children form a line, arms bent at their sides, and move like a train. They can move in a circle or up and down the length of the room.

Play the drum with tempo changes as for activity 10 above. Call "Toot! Toot!" with your voice to slow the train to a stop (or play "Toot! Toot!" on the piano).

The "train" can make several runs, with a different head of the line as "driver."

Story Time

Read the story aloud. Then read it aloud again as the individual parts are carried out in movement and song by the children. One or any number of children can take an individual part.

Characters
Voice Fairy
The Big Black Train
The Little Bird
Train Riders

It was time for the Voice Fairy to give out voices. The Big Black Train waited patiently. The little bird perched quietly on a ledge.

"Oh dear," said the Voice Fairy. "My boxes are all mixed up. Try this one," she said to the train.

"Chirp, chirp" said the Train, way up high.

(The Train says "Chirp, Chirp" way up high.)

Everyone laughed and laughed. Of course, that was the *Bird's* voice!

The Bird took its voice and sang merrily as it flew about. "Chirp, chirp, chirp," we heard.

(The Little Bird flies about as it sings "Chirp, Chirp" way up high.)

"Maybe this one is yours," the Voice Fairy said to the Train.

Play the drum:

 *etc.*

"Toot! Toot!" called the Train, way down low.

(The Train calls "Toot! Toot!" way down low.)

That was his voice, all right. He could hardly wait to start. Everyone got aboard the Train. They sang the "Toot! Toot!" song.

Play on the piano or a pitched instrument as all sing:

Play the drum:

Then the train began to move. Slowly, at first, then faster and faster, it sped down the track. And from far away once more we heard, "T-O-O-T! T-O-O-T!"

(All get in a line to make a train. It starts slowly and then moves faster and faster till it's out of sight.)

Call "Toot! Toot!" as the train moves away.

The End

Lesson 6

Who Will Go?

Allegretto

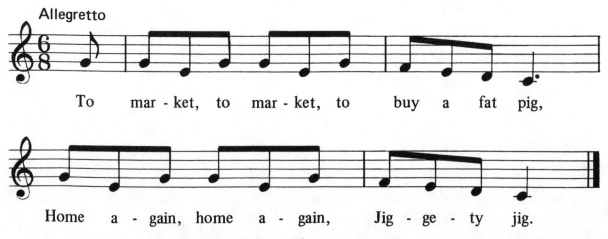

To mar - ket, to mar - ket, to buy a fat pig,

Home a - gain, home a - gain, Jig - ge - ty jig.

Lesson 6
WHO WILL GO?

1   Some day we might have to go to the market to buy a pig. This would be a good song to sing on the way. Listen—

Sing the song and teach it to the children.

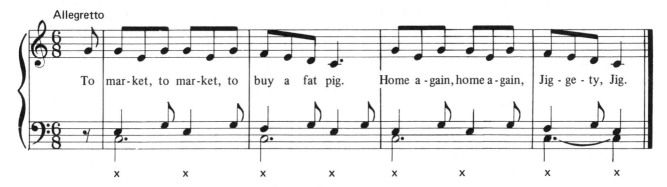

2   Give rhythm sticks to all the children.

Good. In the first part of the song we're going to the market. (Benjy), will you show us how you go to market to buy a fat pig while we sing?

Everyone sings "To market, to market, to buy a fat pig," while (Benjy) moves in any rhythm he wishes.

(Amy), will you show us how you come home while we all sing?

Everyone sings "Home again, home again, jiggety, jig," while (Amy) moves in any rhythm she wishes.

(The children who are singing can also play the rhythm sticks. Encourage the playing of the sticks on the beat, marked *x*.)

3   Who will sing the part of the song that goes to market?

Have two children stand in front. Each sings only the first or second part of the song.

Give other children turns, in sets of two.

4   We have a wagon to carry the pig home. But what will pull the wagon?

Give as many children as possible a turn to show what will pull the wagon.

Have the child initiate the movement in his or her own tempo. After he or she is moving, you can accompany the movements by playing lightly on the drum.

Any choices are acceptable: ponies that walk or gallop, donkeys, etc.

When it seems desirable, have all the children join in with one child's choice.

5   We might meet a friend on the road. Maybe our friend is going *very slowly*. Who could it be?

Probable responses: elephant, slow-moving cat, turtle.

Give individual children a turn to suggest and show the slow-moving animal.

Have the child initiate the movement in his or her own tempo, as in activity 4 above. Again, after he or she is moving, you can accompany the movements by playing lightly on the drum.

42

Other children can join in with the individual child when it seems desirable.

6   If we want to go very fast, we'll need a truck with a motor. (Benjy), show us how you would come home with the pig in your truck.

(Benjy) initiates going very fast in his own way. After he is moving, you can accompany his movements by playing lightly on the drum.

Call for other suggestions for fast ways to go, such as train or plane. Also ask for suggestions for a fast-moving friend they might meet on the way, like a race horse or a flying bird.

When desired, other children can join in with the individual child.

7

All the children are seated.

Let's sing our song *very slowly*, like the turtle moves. We can swing too, like this—

Show a long swing from side to side as you sing very slowly.

←──── To   market, to ────→
←──── market, to   buy a fat ────→
←──── pig.   Home again, ────→
←──── home again,   Jiggety ────→
←──── Jig.

Now all the children can sing and swing with you.

8   Now let's sing like a fast-moving bird. We'll swing, too. Like this—

Show a short swing from side to side as you sing quickly and lightly.

←To   market, to →
←market, to   buy a fat →
←pig.   Home again, →
←home again,   Jiggety →
←Jig.

9

Write this on the chalkboard in large notes:

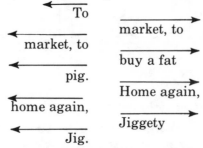

These are the music signs for "Jiggety Jig." (Benjy), come to the board and point to the notes while you say "Jig-ge-ty Jig."

Give other children a chance to do the same.

10

Give each child a handball.

At the market, there was a show for all the people. A juggler showed what he could do with a ball. Let's do the same.

First, have the children practice passing the ball from one hand to the other when you say "Pass."

Then have everyone sing "To Market" while passing the ball from one hand to the other.

Encourage the children to place the balls in their hands with the beat of the song (marked *x* in the song).

11 Sometimes the juggler went very fast and sometimes he went very slowly. Like this—

Pass the ball and sing with the children, very fast.

Or this—

Pass the ball and sing with the children very slowly.
Keep the hands closer together for *fast* and farther apart for *slow*.

12 At the end of the show, the music played so that everyone could take hands with a partner and swing. Sometimes they sang, too.

Have each child face a partner, holding hands, and swing their arms from side to side. Encourage swinging on the beat (*x*) but a general response is sufficient.

As you play the song, have the children swing without singing. Then play again as they swing and sing.

Story Time

Read the story aloud to the children. Then read it aloud again as the individual parts are carried out in movement and song by the children. One or any number of children can take an individual part.

Characters
The Robin
The Turtle
The Pony

Once upon a time, a Robin, a Turtle, and a Pony wanted to go on a journey together.

The Robin said, "When I fly, I go very fast." And he flew all around the wood where they were talking.

(The Robin flies around.)

Play the drum:

etc.

Then the Turtle said, "You see how slowly I go. I don't think I could keep up with you." And he went to the nearest tree and back again to show his friends how he must travel.

(The Turtle moves slowly on the ground.)

Play the drum slowly:

etc.

The Pony spoke next. "I can gallop fast or slow," he said, and he galloped in a large circle. Round and round he went.

(The Pony gallops in a large circle.)

Play the drum for gallop:

etc.

The Pony spoke again. "Perhaps we cannot travel together," he said, "but I know something we can all do right here. Let's sing a song."

So they sang:

Play as all sing:

They all liked that.

The End

Lesson 7

Mr. Rabbit in the Country

Moderate

Hop!   Hop!   Hop!   Hop!

Here I come, here I come, here I come home.

Lesson 7
MR. RABBIT IN THE COUNTRY

1   **This is a good time for walking in the country. Will you walk with the music? Afterwards you can tell us what you saw on the way.**

Play Record 41-6095 S4B2 (Piano No. 35).

2   The children are seated.

  (Amy), what did you see as you were walking?

Give individual children time to tell what they saw on the way. Probable responses: birds, squirrels, rabbits, a cow, ponies, a river.

3   **One of the rabbits you saw tells a story like this—**

Show the finger play and teach it to the children.

Two long ears I have to hear,
When Mr. Farmer's coming near,
Hop, hop, hop, I will stop
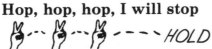
Hop, hop, hop, I will stop.
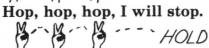

4   **That's good. Be sure to practice this at home. Then we can do it again here. Now we can hop like Mr. Rabbit. He has to be sure to stop when he hears the farmer, so let me see you stop, too, when the drum stops.**

Play for hops with the drum.

Play a short group of hops—wait—another short group of hops—wait—and so on.

5   The children are seated.

  Mr. Rabbit is glad to come home, too. He sings about it like this—

Sing the song and teach it to the children.

6 The children are seated.

Here is Mr. Rabbit's home on the piano.

Show middle C on the piano or xylophone.

C

(Benjy), will you sing and play "I am home" on middle C?

Give other children a turn to do the same. Help them if necessary.
For very young children, cover both sides of the keyboard with cardboard, leaving only one middle octave open, from G to G.

7 Mr. Rabbit comes home from different places. One time he came home like this—

Demonstrate.

(Play.)

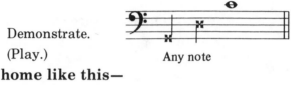

Any note

Another time he came home like this—

Demonstrate.

(Play.)

Any note

Of course, he always comes back to the same home. (Amy), will you show us how Mr. Rabbit came home one day?

Give as many children as possible a turn to play. Any notes are acceptable for "I come," but "home" must be middle C.

8 Mr. Rabbit is in the field again. You can hop with the hops in the song. When you hear the song come home, see how quickly you can get down into your hole on the floor. Then you can come out and hop again.

Play:

Coming home

Repeat as many times as desirable. Vary the length of "hop" measures before playing "coming home."

9 Mr. Rabbit asked all his bird friends to come hear his story. You can fly now, too.

Play Record 41-6088 S5B3 (Piano No. 1) as the children "fly" like birds.

Story Time

Read the story aloud to the children. Then read it aloud again as the individual parts are carried out in movement and song by the children. One or any number of children can take an individual part.

Characters
Mr. Rabbit
Other Rabbits
Birds

Mr. Rabbit liked to watch the TV. But one day something went wrong with all the TV sets in the neighborhood.

"We're lucky we know how to sing and act ourselves," he said. He invited his friends to come to his house.

The Rabbits from down the way were happy to visit. One by one, they hopped in.

(The Rabbits hop in.)

Play the drum:

The Birds from the nearby wood flew in, too.

(The Birds fly in.)

Play the drum:

♫ ♫ ♫ ♫ *etc.*

Everyone sat down in a large circle.

(Everyone sits down in a large circle.)

Now Mr. Rabbit stood in the middle and recited the finger play that he knew.

(Mr. Rabbit recites.)

Two long ears I have to hear,

When Mr. Farmer's coming near,

Hop, hop, hop, I will stop

HOLD

Hop, hop, hop, I will stop.

HOLD

"That was good," called out the Rabbits and the Birds. "What else can you do?"

So Mr. Rabbit sang the "Hop, hop" song.

Play as Mr. Rabbit sings:

Hop! Hop! Hop! Hop! Here I come, here I come, here I come home.

Everyone liked it so much that they wanted to learn it, too, and before they went home they could all sing it. It sounded very fine, like this—

(Song as above)

Play as above as all sing.

The End

Lesson 8

The Three Bears
at Music School

Moderate

Who ate my por - ridge? Who ate it up?

Who ate my por - ridge? Who ate it up?

(Spoken) "Who ate it up? Who ate it up?"

Lesson 8
THE THREE BEARS AT MUSIC SCHOOL

1   Draw three drumsticks on the chalkboard—small, medium, and large sizes.

I think this is a good day to go visit the Three Bears.
(Benjy), will you play the drum to show us one of the Bears walking outside his house? Then tell us which Bear you played, and point to the drumstick on the board that is his.

Give individual children a turn to play the drum for one of the Bears walking, then to point to the drumstick for that Bear.
Encourage very strong playing for Papa Bear, medium strong playing for Mama Bear, and very soft playing for Baby Bear.

2   **Papa Bear and Mama Bear had a lot to do every day. What were some of the things they did?**

Possible responses: gather berries, chop wood for a fire, find nuts.

Sometimes Baby Bear played with the squirrels while Mama Bear and Papa Bear were busy.
You can be any one of the Bears now while the music plays.

Have the children move freely.
Play Record 41-6089 S7B1 (Piano No. 10).

3   **The game Baby Bear liked best of all was called "Find the Honey Jar." Papa Bear would hide the honey jar. Then he played the drum while Mama and Baby Bear went looking. When they were near the honey jar, he played strongly. If they were looking in the wrong place, he played very softly. Let's play the game now.**

Ask the children to close their eyes while you hide a small jar. When the jar is hidden, the children can open their eyes and look for the jar.
Play the drum, getting louder if the children are near the jar and softer if they are farther away.
Have the children take turns in small groups. They should "work together" (moving together) to find the jar.

4   **That was fun. Here is another game the Bears liked.**

Place two chairs in opposite corners. One is the Papa chair and the other is the Baby chair.
When the music is low and strong, the children walk around the Papa Bear chair.
When the music is high and soft, the children walk around the Baby Bear chair.

50

Alternate playing between the high and low music.

5   In our story the Three Bears learn to sing words instead of speaking them. Like this—

Sing instead of speaking: "Who ate my porridge?"
Give individual children turns to sing after you, either "Who ate my porridge?" or "Who ate it up?"

Any effort to use a singing voice rather than a speaking voice is good.

6   There was one song all the Bears sang together.

Sing the song and teach it to the children.

(Spoken) "Who ate it up?   Who ate it up?"

7   Good. Now you can run like the Three Bears coming home from Music School.
Play Record 41-6092 S5B1 (Piano No. 9).

Story Time

Read the story aloud. Then read it aloud again as the individual parts are carried out in movement and song by the children. One or any number of children can take an individual part.

Characters
Papa Bear
Mama Bear
Baby Bear
The Music Teacher
All the Bears at the
    school

Once upon a time the Three Bears—Papa Bear, Mama Bear, and Baby Bear—went to see a movie about Jack and the Beanstalk.

Instead of speaking, like you and I do when we talk to one another, everyone in the story *sang* his or her words. Even the Giant sang:

The Three Bears liked that. "Let's do the same," Papa Bear said. "We can tell about the time Goldilocks came to our house. But first we must go to Music School to learn to sing." So that's what they did.

The Music Teacher sang to Papa Bear and Mama Bear:

Play on the piano or pitched instrument as the Music Teacher sings:

(Music Teacher sings.)

Papa and Mama Bear sang the same. Now the Music Teacher sang to Baby Bear:

Play as the Music Teacher sings.

(Music Teacher sings.)

Baby Bear said, "Who ate my porridge?" "No, no," said the Music Teacher. She sang again.

"Who ate it up?" said Baby Bear, a little louder.

"No, no, listen once more," said the Music Teacher. She sang again. And now Baby Bear sang just like the teacher.

Play on the piano or pitched instrument as Baby Bear sings.

(Baby Bear sings.)

One day the Three Bears and all their school friends sang the whole song. Everyone liked that.

Play as the Three Bears
and all the Bears at
school sing:

Moderate

Who ate my por-ridge? Who ate it up? Who ate my por-ridge? Who ate it up?

(Spoken) "Who ate it up? Who ate it up?"

The End

Lesson 9

The Farmer in the Dell

Allegretto

The Farm - er in the dell, _____ the

Farm - er in the dell, _____ Hi Ho, the

der - ry - o, the Farm - er in the dell. _____

54

Lesson 9
THE FARMER IN THE DELL

1   Yesterday I read a story about a farmer. It told how every day he walked around on his farm to see how the corn was growing.

(Amy), will you show us how the farmer walked?

Have one child initiate walking in his or her own way and then all the children join in the walking. Then play the music as they continue to walk. Play Record 41-6095 S4B2 (Piano No. 35).

2   You looked like really good farmers. Did anyone see something special on the way?

Possible responses: a rabbit hopping, birds flying, a pony galloping, a cow.

Give individual children a turn to show their choices in free movement. Other children can join in.

3   The farmer thinks the birds might eat his corn. He makes a scarecrow. It looks like this—

Draw a picture like this on the chalkboard.

Tell how the scarecrow, made of straw and old clothes to look like a man, keeps the birds away.

4

Draw a scarecrow without arms on the board.

Have one child add the arms.

Later we'll all draw scarecrows in our books.

5   (Benjy), will you be a scarecrow in the field now? Everyone else is a flying bird. The music tells when the birds see the scarecrow and stop, and when they fly again.

Play the drum with a running rhythm (♩♩) as the children fly like birds.

Wait between intervals of playing, as the birds see the scarecrow and stop. One child can stand still as the scarecrow.

Or play Record 41-6094 S1B2 (Piano No. 33). Stop the music at intervals.

6   Good. Scarecrows don't always look the same. Sometimes they get a little droopy in the rain. Then, when the sun comes out, they get dry and stand up straight. Listen, I think he's droopy now. Show me how he looks.

The children are "droopy" scarecrows as you play on the piano or another pitched instrument.

Now he feels better.

Play, as the children show the scarecrow "feeling better":

How does he feel now?

Play either mood, as the children respond by the difference in their posture.

7
The children are seated.

Here is the farmer's special song. Listen—

Sing the song and teach it to the children. (Tell them what a *dell* is—a field where the land is sheltered.)

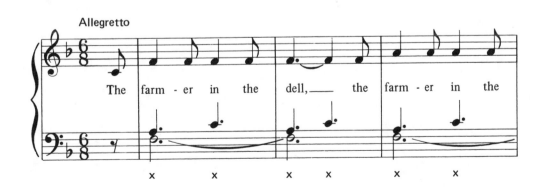

8   (Benjy), will you play the rhythm sticks while we clap and sing?

> Give individual children a turn with the rhythm sticks as everyone sings and claps. Encourage clapping and playing the rhythm sticks on the beat, marked *x* in the song.

9

> Draw a walking note on the chalkboard: ♩

This is a music sign that tells us the farmer is walking. We call it a walking note.

> Point out the round bottom, like a ball, with a stick that is helpful for walking.
>
> Give all the children a turn to put the walking note on the board, or to add the stick (or stem) to a bottom already drawn.
>
> *Example:*   •   •   •

10

> Have note cards (♫ ♩ ♩) face up on the floor, with walking note cards for each child.

As soon as everyone picks out a walking note card, we can sing our song and walk like the Farmer in the Dell.

> (Pick up the cards remaining on the floor.)
>
> Have all the children sing and walk, as you play the song as in activity 7 above.
>
> Or play Record 41-6152 S5B1.

Story Time

Characters
The Farmer
The Scarecrow
Birds
Rabbit
Neighbors

Play the drum:

♫ ♫ ♫ ♫ *etc.*

Play the drum:

♪ ♪ ♪ ♪ *etc.*

Read the story aloud. Then read it aloud again as the individual parts are carried out in movement and song by the children. One or any number of children can take an individual part.

(The Scarecrow is standing in the field as the story is read the second time.)

It was time for the Farmer to take his walk. In the fields he would see the Birds flying.

(The Birds fly.)

Maybe he would see a Rabbit hopping along.

(A Rabbit hops.)

Of course, the Scarecrow would be standing where the corn was planted.

As he was leaving the house, the Farmer said, "I think I'll take my walking note along for company. Where is it? It must be in the big box with the other cards."

The Farmer pulled out the cards one by one.

(The Farmer pulls out the cards one by one.)

⨅ **"Is it this one? No.** 𝅝 **Is it this one? No.**

𝅘𝅥 **Here it is!"**

He held the card as he walked along.

(The Farmer walks along.)

Play the drum:

♩ ♩ ♩ ♩ ♩ *etc.*

Play on the piano or another pitched instrument as all walk and sing:

On the way, he met his Neighbors. They all walked together as they sang the Farmer's special song. What a good time they had!

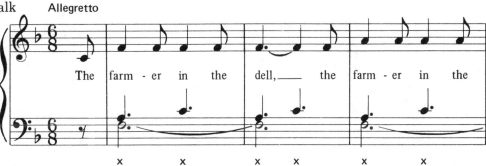

The End

Lesson 10

My Pony

Allegro

I'm rid - ing on a po - ny, I'm rid - ing on a

po - ny, I'm rid - ing on a po - ny, and now we'll STOP!

Lesson 10
MY PONY

1   Give all the children wrist bells.

Let's be galloping ponies this morning. (Benjy), will you be the lead pony and start first? Call out "Whoa" when you come to a red light, and "Go" when the light turns green.

Have one child initiate the galloping. Then the other children join in. You can follow their movement with the galloping rhythm on the drum:

Encourage adequate time intervals between "Whoa" and "Go." (Do not play the drum during the intervals.) Play Record 41-6095 S4B1 (Paino No. 34) without stops.

2   The children are seated.

Let's make the galloping sound on our knees, like this—

Tap with your hands, palms down on your knees, in the galloping rhythm:

♪ ♩

Left Right

♪ ♩

Left Right

♪ ♩

Left Right

Have the children do this with you. Some might want to add "Giddy-up, giddy-up" as they tap.

3   Give the children rhythm sticks.

Good. Now the pony is walking. (Benjy), will you be the walking pony while we play our rhythm sticks and say "Walk, walk, walk, walk"?

Have one child walk as the pony while everyone else plays the rhythm sticks in a walking rhythm and says "Walk, walk, walk, walk," and so on.

4   This time all our ponies can gallop or walk. The drum will tell you what to do.

Play the drum either for the galloping rhythm (♩♪), or for walking (♩ ♩). Have all the children follow the drum.

♩. = ♩

♩ ♪ = ♩

5   The children are seated.

This galloping pony song has a special ending. Listen—

Sing the song and teach it to the children. The children can clap at "Now we'll stop," as a substitute for the drum while learning the song.

60

I'm rid - ing on a po - ny, I'm rid - ing on a

po - ny, I'm rid - ing on a po - ny, and NOW WE'LL STOP.

Drum   x   x   x

6   Give individual children a turn to play the drum with "Now we'll stop," as everyone sings.

7 **How many times do we sing "I'm riding on a pony?"**

Sing the song with the children, as everyone counts on extended fingers to find the three instances of "I'm riding on a pony."

Have three children stand side by side. Each sings "I'm riding on a pony" once, and then the drummer and all the children join in at "Now we'll stop."

8   Draw the galloping notes on the board:

This is the music sign for galloping. Who will copy it on the chalkboard?

Give individual children their turns to draw the galloping notes on the board.

9   Have note cards face up on the floor with enough galloping and walking

cards for each child.

Everyone can find a galloping card for himself or herself. Then we'll have a good gallop.

Pick up the cards remaining on the floor.

Play on the piano or another pitched instrument, as the children gallop, or play Record 41-6095 S4B1 (Piano No. 34).

10 If I tap you on the shoulder, exchange your galloping card for a walking note card.

> Spread the remaining note cards out again, and have half the children exchange their galloping cards for walking note cards.
> Pick up the remaining cards from the floor.

11 We have a stable for the walking pony and one for the galloping pony in these two corners.

> Show them the "stables" at opposite corners of the room.
> The galloping pony and the walking pony each come out for their own music, in their own rhythm, and go back when the music changes.
> Play the drum and alternate between the gallop and the walk. Vary the length of time between each rhythm.

Story Time

> Read the story aloud. Then read it aloud again as the individual parts are carried out in movement and song by the children. One or many children can take an individual part.

Characters
The Walking Pony
The Galloping Pony
The People at the Horse
  Show
The Drummer

Play the drum for
galloping:

(Both ponies are in opposite corners of the room.)

Once upon a time there was a Galloping Pony. Galloping is what he did best. Every year he looked forward to the Horse Show. Then he could come out proudly as the galloping music played, like this—

(Galloping Pony comes out and gallops, then goes back to his corner.)

His cousin was a Walking Pony. He always listened especially well for the walking music, starting and stopping just right, like this—

62

Play the drum for walking:

♩ ♩ ♩ ♩ ♩ *etc.*

(Walking Pony comes out and walks, then goes back to his corner.)

This year they were going to do something different at the Horse Show. Each pony would come out for his own music, as they did every year, but at the end everyone would sing a special song.

What excitement there was on the day of the show! The two ponies were listening so hard they could feel their ears wiggle.

The music began. The right pony was out the minute he heard it.

Play the drum:

♩ ♪♩ ♪ *etc.*

(Galloping Pony gallops out.)

A change!

Play the drum:

♩ ♩ ♩ ♩ *etc.*

(Walking Pony walks out and Galloping Pony goes back to his corner.)

Another change!

Play the drum:

♩ ♪♩ ♪ *etc.*

(Galloping Pony gallops out and Walking Pony goes back to his corner.)

A change again!

Play the drum:

♩ ♩ ♩ ♩ *etc.*

(Walking Pony walks out and Galloping Pony goes back to his corner.)

The music stopped.

The audience said it was a super horse show. Now everyone came together to sing the pony song, and (Benjy) played the drum just right at "Now we'll stop."

Play on the piano or another pitched instrument as all sing and (Benjy) plays on the drum.

Allegro

I'm rid-ing on a po - ny, I'm rid-ing on a po - ny, I'm rid-ing on a po - ny, and NOW WE'LL STOP.

Drum   x   x   x

The End

Lesson 11

Tap, Tap, Tap, Tap
or The Cobbler

Allegro

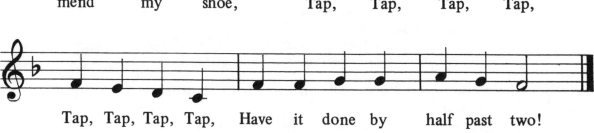

Tap, Tap, Tap, Tap, Tap, Tap, Tap, Tap, Cob - bler, Cob - bler,

mend my shoe, Tap, Tap, Tap, Tap,

Tap, Tap, Tap, Tap, Have it done by half past two!

Lesson 11
TAP, TAP, TAP, TAP
or THE COBBLER

1   **Let's play a good game. Run with the music. If the music stops "high," raise your arms when you stop.**

If the music stops "low," bend over as you stop.

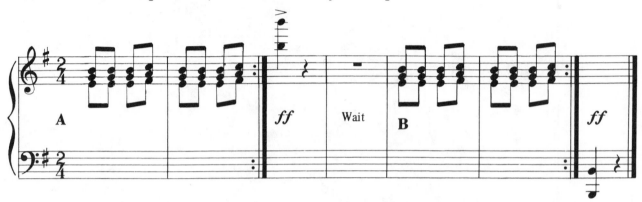

Alternate playing between A and B: A A, A B, B B, and so on.

2   The children are seated.

That was good.
On my way to school, I looked in the window of a cobbler's shop.

Tell the children what a cobbler is.

I could see that some shoes were waiting to be mended. But right in the front was a fine pair of walking shoes with brand new heels. (Benjy), will you show us one way the walking shoes could go?

Have one child initiate the movement in his or her own tempo. As he or she moves, you can accompany with the drum.
If desirable, other children can join in.

3   **(Amy), the walking shoes might step in different ways. Maybe they went faster.**

Have one child initiate the movement. As he or she moves, you can accompany with the drum.
If desirable, other children can join in.

4   **Sometimes the walking shoes go very, very slowly, and sometimes they go very, very fast.**

Divide the children into two groups in opposite corners of the room. One group comes out and walks only when you play very fast, and the other group comes out only when you play very slowly. Each group goes back to its corner upon hearing any tempo but its own.
After the groups have responded several times, have the children change parts.
Play the drum, either very fast or very slowly. Short intervals of responses are better than long intervals.

5   **We can all do the heavy boots. I think they must belong to a farmer. They take a really big, strong step.**

Play Record 41-6090 S1B2 (Piano No. 19).

6   It's fun to try out the dancing slippers. Sometimes they have to do a stamping dance that goes "Stamp, stamp, stamp—Stamp, stamp, stamp," Listen now. I think you will hear where the dancer stamps.

Say the "Stamp, stamp, stamp" as you play on the piano or another pitched instrument.

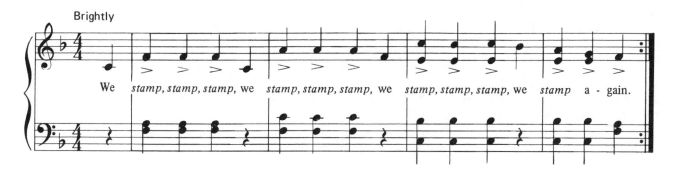

Play again, as the children stamp with you at Stamp, stamp, stamp" (with either foot or alternating).

7   Sometimes the dancing slippers go lightly on tiptoe, like fairies and elves.

Play Record 41-6089 S8B1 (Piano No. 12).

8   Next time you take your shoes to the cobbler, you can sing this song to him. Listen—

Sing the song and teach it to the children.

9   The cobbler knows the song, too. He sings as he hammers. Like this—

Make a "cobbler's bench" with a low table, a block, and a rhythm stick.
Sing as you hammer on the beat (marked *x* in the song).
Sometimes all the children can sing with the cobbler.
Give as many children as possible the chance to be the cobbler.

10   Write the notes for "Have it done by half-past two" on the chalkboard, written large.

These are the music signs for the last part of our song.

(Show.) Point to the notes as you sing. Give a turn to two or three children to do the same.

11 The dancing shoes like to swing with the song. (Benjy), will you be the cobbler hammering while we all sing and dance?

Have the children take partners, face each other, and hold hands. They swing their arms from side to side as everyone sings:

Tap, tap, ⟶

tap, tap ⟵

Tap, tap, ⟶

tap, tap, ⟵

Cobbler ⟶

Cobbler, ⟵

Mend my ⟶

Shoe ⟵   etc.

Play as for activity 8 above.

Story Time

Characters
Walking Shoes
Boots
Dancing Shoes
A Slipper

Play the drum:

♩ ♩ ♩ ♩ ♩ *etc.*

Play the drum:

♩ ♩ ♩ ♩ *etc.*

Play the drum:

♪ ' ♪ ' ♪ ' ♪ ' *etc.*

Play as all sing the song, "Tap Tap," and the Dancing Shoes swing: *(song below)*

Play as all sing, the Dancing Shoes swing, the Slipper plays the wood block, (marked *x* in the song) and the boots swing their arms.

Read the story aloud to the children. Then read it aloud again as the individual parts are carried out in movement and song by the children.

The cobbler had worked hard all day. He was glad to go home. For a little while it was very quiet in the shop. Then the Walking Shoes said, "I wonder how my new heels are. I'll just try them out."

(Walking Shoes walk.)

"Oh, we feel good," they said.

"How do *we* look?" called out a pair of heavy Boots as they took big steps up and down.

(Heavy Boots take big steps.)

"Fine," said everyone. The Boots really did look fine.

The pink Dancing Shoes tiptoed into the room from the corner.

(Dancing Shoes tiptoe in.)

"Would you like us to dance?" they asked. So everyone sang the cobbler's song while the Dancing Shoes did a beautiful swing from side to side.

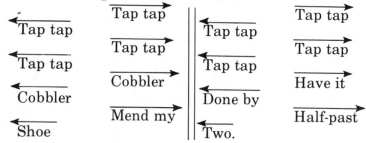

Now all the shoes sang the cobbler's song again, while the Walking Shoes walked, the Dancing Shoes danced, and a Slipper played the wood block. The Boots stood in front and swung their arms from side to side. It went like this—

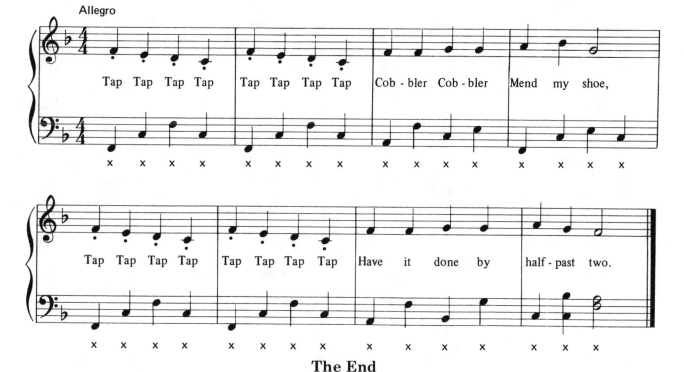

The End

Lesson 12

Gobble Gobble

Brightly

See the tur - key, he is run - ning

on Thanks - giv - ing Day. Gob - ble, gob - ble,

gob - ble, gob - ble, That is what he'll say.

Lesson 12
GOBBLE GOBBLE

1   Here's our turkey in the barnyard. Will you run with him while I play the drum?
When you don't hear the drum, he's just looking around. You can look around then,
too.

Play the drum for running in short spurts:
Wait in between for the turkey to look around.

2   The children are seated.

The turkey has many friends in the barnyard. You can be one of the friends he goes
to visit.

Play the drum as you tell who you are, and then speak a little in your own
language. Like this—

(Show.) Speak as you play the drum:

"I am the cow."   (in any rhythm)
"Moo, moo."   (without drum)

Give individual children a turn. Any animal is possible—sheep, horse,
chicken, duck, pig, rooster.

3   Give all the children rhythm sticks.

Our turkey plays this game with another turkey. I'll play first, then you answer me
exactly the same way.

Play on a drum as you say:

Gob - ble   gob - ble   gob - ble

Have the children repeat exactly the same. Then play on the drum as
you say:

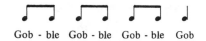

Gob - ble   Gob

The children repeat exactly the same. Continue, one line at a time.

Gob - ble   Gob - ble   Gob - ble   Gob

Gob - ble   Gob - ble   Gob - ble   Gob - ble

Gob - ble   Gob - ble   Gob - ble

The same rhythm can be done several times in succession.

70

4   Good. There's always a song for Thanksgiving. But first let's all sing up the ladder to 5 and then down. Then I'll sing the song for you.

> Sing with the children. (Play also, if you wish, on the piano or another pitched instrument.) Have the children sing the numbers 1, 2, 3, 4, 5 (going up), and then 5, 4, 3, 2, 1 (going down).
>
> Have the children raise and lower one arm while singing. Repeat once or twice.

5
> Sing the song and teach it to the children.

6   Let's make the running sound on our knees while we sing "Gobble, gobble, gobble, gobble, gobble, that is what he'll say."

> Show, singing and tapping on your knees:
> Gobble, Gobble, Gobble, Gobble
>   L R L R L R L R
> That is what he'll s_ _ _a_ _y_ _ _
>   L R L R L R L R
> Repeat as all the children sing and tap with you.

7   This is the music sign for running.

> Draw large running notes on the chalkboard:

> Call attention to the two notes together, for running. Then have several children copy the running notes on the board.

8
> Place varied note cards face up on the floor or any other surface, with enough running note cards for each child.

Everyone can pick a running note card, and then we'll all be the turkey running on Thanksgiving Day.

> Play Record 41-6092 S5B3 (Piano No. 17).

Story Time

Characters
Baby Turkey
Mother Turkey
Turkey Relatives
Duck House (two
up-ended chairs)

Play the drum:

♫ ♫ ♫ ♫ *etc.*

Play the drum:

♩ ♩ ♩ ♩ *etc.*

Play the drum:

♫ ♫ ♫ ♫ *etc.*

Play the song "Gobble Gobble" as Baby Turkey, Mother Turkey, and all the Relatives sing:

Read the story aloud to the children. Then read it aloud again as the individual parts are carried out in movement and song by the children. One or any number of children can take an individual part.

Mr. and Mrs. Turkey and their children lived happily on Mr. Jones's farm. Every day Baby Turkey played in the barnyard. His favorite game was to hide till he was found by Mother Turkey.

One time Baby Turkey was running all around looking as usual for a place to hide.

(Baby Turkey runs around looking for a place to hide.)

When he saw the duck house, he said, "I'll hide here. When Mother comes to look for me, I'll go 'Quack, quack' like a duck, Mother will think there's a *duck* here, not *me*."

(Baby Turkey hides in the duck house.)

In a little while Mother came to find Baby Turkey. "Gobble, gobble," she called, as she walked everywhere.

(Mother Turkey walks everywhere.)

Just as she was about to go into the duck house, Baby Turkey called out.

(Baby Turkey calls out "Quack, quack!")

Mother Turkey went by, thinking of course that a duck was inside. Soon it was almost dark. Poor Baby Turkey could not find the way home. He ran here and there.

(Baby Turkey runs here and there.)

"Gobble, gobble," he called as loud as he could.

(Baby Turkey calls, "Gobble, gobble.")

"Gobble, gobble," he called again, even louder.

(Baby Turkey calls louder, "Gobble, gobble.")

Luckily, Mother Turkey heard him. She came to get him. Baby Turkey never played *that* game again!

The next day was Thanksgiving and Baby Turkey was happy to see all his Relatives and to sing with them.

Brightly

See the tur-key, he is run-ning on Thanks-giv-ing Day,

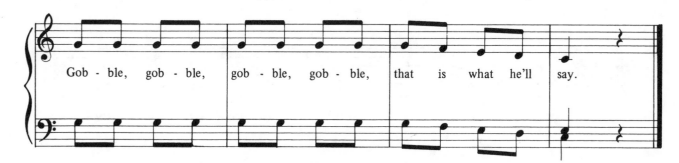

Gob-ble, gob-ble, gob-ble, gob-ble, that is what he'll say.

Lesson 13

Happy Birthday to You

Brightly

Hap - py   Birth - day   to   you,   Hap - py

Birth - day   to   you,   Hap - py   Birth - day   dear

__   __   Hap - py   Birth - day   to   you.

Stand up,   stand up,   stand up and make us   a   bow!

Lesson 13
HAPPY BIRTHDAY TO YOU

1   Today we're going to get ready for (Benjy's) birthday party. Everyone will want to sing then. Let's go over the songs we know.

> Have the children sing several songs learned thus far. See how many they can remember without prompting.
>
> One song can be done while walking, another while swinging arms with a partner, another with rhythm sticks, and so on.

2   The children are seated.

This is a good time to make a cake.

> Have the children act out putting all the ingredients into a bowl to be mixed.

Now we'll mix it really well. The music will help you.

> The children "mix the cake" as the music plays.
>
> Play record 41-6091 S4B3 (Piano No. 18).

3   While the cake is baking, let's see if we have enough candles. (Benjy), listen and tell me how many candles light up when I play.

> Play any number from 1 to 5 on the piano or a pitched instrument.

> Give other children a turn to answer for different numbers.

4   (Amy), will you make three candles light up on a black note on the piano (or on a note on another pitched instrument)?

> Give other children a turn to play any number from 1 to 5.

5   Now we have five candles that light up when I play their number. Then their light goes out, too.

> Have five children, numbered 1 to 5, stand in a line facing front, their heads looking downward and their arms at their sides.
>
> As you play going up from 1 to 5, each child in turn raises his or her arms overhead in a triangle to make the candle light, and looks upward.
>
> Play rather slowly, with different time intervals between each "candle."
>
> Then, as you play coming down from 5 to 1, each child in turn lowers his or her arms to the original position.

> You can do the same activity with another group of five children. This time, each can sing his or her number while raising or lowering his or her arms.

6   Good. We'll learn the birthday song now. It goes like this—

> Sing the song and teach it to the children.

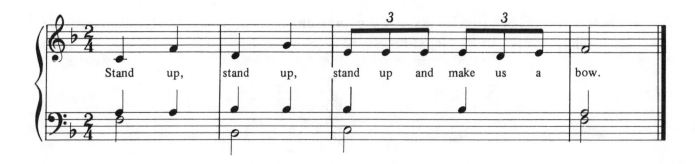

7 **Everyone will have a birthday some time this year, so let's all practice making a bow while everyone else sings that part of the song.**

> Play and sing as all the children sing "Stand up, stand up, stand up and make us a bow."
>
> Give as many children as possible a turn to stand and make a bow. (Others will practice the next time the song is done.)
>
> A simple bow from the waist is sufficient.

8 **(Benjy), would you like to play "Happy Birthday" to a friend on the drum?**

> Give individual children a turn to say and play "Happy Birthday" on the drum. Before he or she plays, have each child tell whose birthday it is. Encourage them to play softly or loudly as appropriate (for example, very softly to a tiny mouse, very loudly to the big dog down the street).

9 **Maybe there will be games to play at the birthday party. This is a wonderful game called "Musical Chairs."**

> Place a row of chairs in a line, facing alternate ways, one less than the number of children taking part. The children walk around the chairs as the music plays. When the music stops, they sit down on the nearest chair. The child who is without a chair is out.
>
> Take one chair from the row of chairs, and the game resumes.
>
> Play Record 41-6091 S3B4 (Piano No. 16).

Play the music in rather short intervals, stopping at unexpected places. If too many children make the game too long, it can be stopped when a certain number of children are out, making all the rest winners.

10 That was fun.

Suppose you could have an animal friend for a birthday present. Close your eyes and think about which one you would want ... Now open your eyes and, when I call your name, tell us your wish.

Benjy made the same kind of birthday wish. Listen—

Story Time

Characters
Benjy
Baby Elephant
Giraffe
Pony
Benjy's Friends

Read the story aloud to the children. Then read it aloud again as the individual parts are carried out in movement and song by the children.

(Benjy is lying down.)

The next day would be Benjy's birthday. As he lay down to sleep he closed his eyes and made his birthday wish.

"I wish I could have my friends from the zoo come to live with me." The Birthday Fairy must have heard him because, when he opened his eyes and sat up, he could hardly believe what he saw.

(Benjy sits up.)

Very near his bed were the zoo animals he loved most—the Baby Elephant, the tall Giraffe, and the galloping Pony.

Soon the Pony felt at home and began to gallop. Round and round he went.

(The Pony gallops.)

Play the drum:

♩ ♪ ♩ ♪ *etc.*

The Baby Elephant walked here and there swinging his trunk to see if he could find a corner he liked.

(The Baby Elephant walks.)

Play the drum:

♫ ♩ ♫ ♩ *etc.*

The tall Giraffe went bump, bump, with his head on the ceiling.

(The tall Giraffe goes bump, bump.)

Play the drum:

♩   ♩ *etc.*

How the room shook! "Oh," said Benjy," it doesn't look as though my room is big enough for all of us. What shall I do? Oh, oh." He shook his head from side to side.

(Benjy shakes his head.)

I think the Birthday Fairy heard that, too, because soon Benjy fell asleep, and when he awoke the next morning there was only a basket by his head.

In the basket was a beautiful puppy, just the right size for Benjy. What a happy birthday that was!

All his Friends came to wish him a Happy Birthday, and to sing the Birthday Song.

Play as all Benjy's
Friends sing:

The End

I Can Be
Finger Play

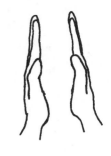

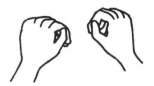

First we're very tall
Then we're very small
Now we're round
just like a ball

'Til we very gently fall
That is all
That is all.

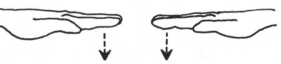

Andante

First we're ver - y tall, then we're ver - y small.

Now we're round just like a ball. 'Til we gent - ly

fall, That is all, That is all.

Lesson 14
I CAN BE

1   There's a little river by my house. Will you run with it? It runs softly, like this—

> Have the children listen and then run softly. Play Record 41-6089 S8B1 (Piano No. 12).

2   You really moved like a river. Now it's winter and the cold winds blow, and the water turns into ... Right! Ice! Cold and very, very hard.

   (Benjy), will you be the wind as it blows around and everyone else is turning into ice?

> Have the children stand (the water is turning into ice) while one child runs as the wind.
> Use your voice for the wind—"Ooooooh, ooooooh, ooooooh"—and play the drum with running notes, getting louder and softer.

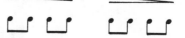

Now I'll go around to see if you're really frozen as hard as ice.

> Feel the children's arms or legs to see if they are really "frozen as hard as ice."

3   The sun is coming out. It's warm. We're getting softer and softer, melting down. Now we can run softly with the river again.

> Use your voice as the children "soften" until they become like water and can run with the river.
> Play Record 41-6089 S8B1. (Piano No. 12).

4   That was good.
   Listen. One of my favorite toys is marching. He's made of wood and is very, very hard. What toy do you think it might be?

> Most children will suggest a wooden soldier.
> Have all the children initiate the movement of walking very stiffly like a wooden toy.
> Then play Record 41-6090 S1B1 (Piano No. 29) as the children continue to walk.

5   A friend of mine lives in my house. He walks on four feet and is very, very soft. Who do you think it is?

> Most children will suggest the cat.
> Have all the children initiate the movement of the cat, walking on hands and feet, softly and slowly.
> Then play Record 41-6096 S5B3 (Piano No. 30), as the children continue to move like cats.

6   Good. Now it's time for a guessing game.

> Have all children look at the song page pictures of the Giant, the Clown, and the Turtle.
> Invite one child to go to the center of the room and stand, move, or gesture like one of the pictures. Ask the other children to guess which picture the child is portraying.
> Give other children a turn.

7   The children are standing, sitting or on the floor.

Now I'm going to let you have some magic dust so we can be lots of different things (very freely).

Have a different child go around to sprinkle the magic dust for each change.

"I'm tall"—stretched high (giraffe, skyscraper, church steeple)
"I'm small"—on floor in a ball (mouse, ball, baby bird)
"I'm cold"—squeezed, frozen looking (snowball, tree in winter, ice cube)
"I'm hot"—loose or active (someone in hot sun, steam kettle)
"I'm hard"—(stone statue, sword, wooden soldier)
"I'm soft"—(pillow, rag doll, custard)
"I'm a balloon getting blown up"—starting small and getting bigger
"I'm an icicle in the sun"—tall and frozen, getting smaller and melting to the ground

8   Good. Let's say what we are on the xylophone.

Speak alone first and then speak with the children: (Start very softly.) "I am getting louder, louder."

Now have one child play the same on the xylophone on any tones, as he or she says the words.

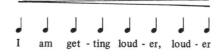

Speak alone first and then speak with the children: (Start very loudly.) "I am getting softer, softer."

Now have one child play the same on the xylophone on any tones, as he or she says the words.

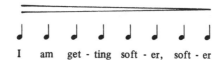

Continue in the same way. One phrase to play is sufficient.

Examples: As the child plays, saying either "I am fast," or "I'm a car."

"I a - - m   s - - l - - o - - w." (I'm a turtle.)
"I am hard." (I'm a statue.)
"I am soft." (I'm a rag doll.)
"I am glad." (I'm a clown.)
"I am sad." (I lost my ball.)
"I am getting faster." (Chug-chug-chugchugchug.)
"I am getting slower." (RRRRRR-rr-r---r---.)

Encourage other choices—"I am putty," or a pillow, or water for soft, or again, just "I am soft."

9   The children are seated.

Our hands are good storytellers, too.

Sing and do the finger play, and teach it to the children.

For your own sense of ease and for more effective teaching of the finger play, it is best to have both the song and the gestures memorized beforehand.

Andante

First we're ver-y tall, then we're ver-y small. Now we're round just

like a ball, 'til we gen-tly fall. That is all, that is all.

10 Good. We'll do it again tomorrow. Now, if we have someone to wave the magic wand, we can all change into elves and fairies when the music plays.

Have all the children move freely like fairies and elves.
Play Record 41-6097 S7B2 (Piano No. 20).

Story Time

Read the story aloud. Then read it aloud again as the individual parts are carried out in movement and song by the children. One or many children can take an individual part.

Characters
A Cat
A Mouse
Players in the Finger Play

Once upon a time a Cat and a Mouse lived on the same block. Now, this Cat was not a very nice cat, and he liked to frighten the Mouse as much as he could. Often, when the Mouse was playing quietly by himself, the Cat would tiptoe up behind him and scare him with a "Yeow!"

One day the Cat boasted to the little Mouse, "I can make myself as big as a tiger," and he grew bigger and bigger and bigger.

(The cat grows bigger and bigger.)

Play the drum from very soft to very loud:

The little Mouse was terrified, but he bravely said, "That is very wonderful. Can you make yourself small, too, as small as a piece of cheese?"

"Of course," said the Cat. And smaller and smaller and smaller he became until he was just as small as a piece of cheese.

(The cat becomes smaller and smaller.)

Play the drum from very loud to very soft:

Play the piano or another pitched instrument as Players sing and do the Finger Play.

I think you know what happened then. That's right, the Mouse ate the cheese and lived happily ever after.

Now every week he went to the Finger Play shows. His favorite was the one about getting small. It went like this:

The End

Lesson 15

It's Raining

**Dutch Folk Song
(adapted)**

Moderato

Pit - ter, pat - ter goes the rain, Fall - ing

on my win - dow pane, Fall - ing, fall - ing down.___

Lesson 15
IT'S RAINING

1   Whenever it rains, Benjy turns to this song in his book.

Sing the song and teach it to the children.

2   I think some big raindrops fell into our song. Let's clap them as we sing.

Clap and sing with the children. (Claps are marked *x* in the song.)
Then play and sing as in activity 1 above, as the children sing and clap.

3   Who will step with me like a big raindrop?

Step with one or two children as you sing. (Steps are marked *x* in the
song.) Then all the children can step in a circle as they sing and you play.
Repeat. Then have the children change directions and repeat again.

4   The children are seated.

Good. We can hear the small raindrops, too. Let's find them together.

Sing the song with the children as in activity 1 while clapping as
marked (*xx*).

**5   Now I'll play the song so you can run like the little raindrops. They're fast and very
light, so run on your toes.**

Play lightly and softly on the piano or another pitched instrument.
When repeating, have the children change direction.

6   The children are seated. Write on the chalkboard:

Here are the music signs for "Falling, falling down." Who will point to the signs with me as we sing?

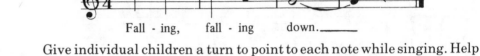

Fall - ing,   fall - ing   down._____

Give individual children a turn to point to each note while singing. Help them if necessary.

7   Let's see how many ways we can sing our song.

Have the children sit on the floor, with legs outstretched and hands on the floor at each side. They swing from side to side while singing the song, first *very* slowly: Since you are facing the children, reverse your swing to show:

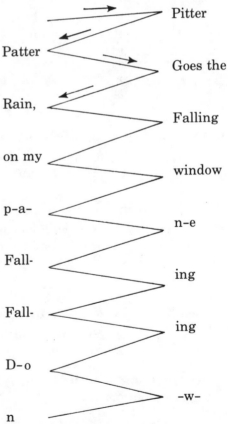

Now do the song and swing in a moderate tempo. Then repeat again in a fast tempo.

Match the length of the swing to the tempo. The faster swing is shorter; the slower swing is longer.

Have individual children suggest and show a tempo that they all do.

8   Draw this on the chalkboard:

This drum has two voices. One says "Rain, rain, go away" very *loudly*. The other says "Rain, rain, go away" very *softly*.

Show the big size of the loud voice in the writing on the board and play on the drum, very loudly, as you say *in a loud voice:*

RAIN, RAIN, GO AWAY
x   x   x   x

Show how the stick is held far from the drum to make the loud sound.

Now show the small size of the soft voice in the writing on the board and play on the drum, very softly, as you say *softly:*

Rain, rain, go away
x   x   x   x

Show how the stick is held close to the drum when playing the soft sound.

Which voice is speaking now?

Play the drum in either voice. Have one child, or all the children, point on the board to the voice played and tell whether it was the loud voice or the soft voice.

9   Now you can each play the voice you like best.

Have one child play and the other children answer to "Which one was it?"

10   Give all the children handballs.

If the rain went away, you could go out to play with your ball. Let's ask the rain to go away.

Have the children pass the ball (on *x*) from one hand to the other as they say:

Rain, rain, go away
x   x   x   x
Come again another day
x   x   x   x

Now have the children repeat, this time in a whisper. The hands are held close—a shorter space because of the softer sound.

Did the rain hear us? We'll ask again, in a louder voice.

Have the children again pass the ball from one hand to the other, saying the verse in a loud voice this time. The hands should be held farther apart. The louder voice uses more space.

Story Time

Read the story aloud. Then read it aloud again as the individual parts are carried out in movement and song by the children. One or any number of children can take an individual part.

Characters
Benjy
Benjy's Friends
Raindrops

It was raining. Benjy liked the rain, but he wanted to bounce his new ball on the sidewalk. He looked out the window. He saw the raindrops go "Pitter patter, pitter patter."

(The Raindrops run.)

Play on the piano or any pitched instrument as the raindrops run:

Now Benjy passed the ball from one hand to the other as he said very softly:

(Benjy speaks as he passes the ball.)

"Rain, rain, go away   *(Hands close*
  x   x   x   x   *together.)*
Come again another day"
  x   x   x   x

It was still raining. "Maybe no one heard," he thought. "I'll ask again, a little louder." He said, very strongly.

(Benjy speaks again louder.)

"RAIN, RAIN, GO AWAY   *(Hands farther*
  x   x   x   x   *apart.)*
COME AGAIN ANOTHER DAY"
  x   x   x   x

What a good surprise! The raindrops were going away.

(The Raindrops run around and then run away.)

Play on the piano or another pitched instrument as above for raindrops running.

Now Benjy could go out with his ball. "Thank you, rain," he said.

All his Friends were outside. They had a good time passing their balls from one hand to the other as they sang the Rain Song.

Play as all sing and
pass the ball:

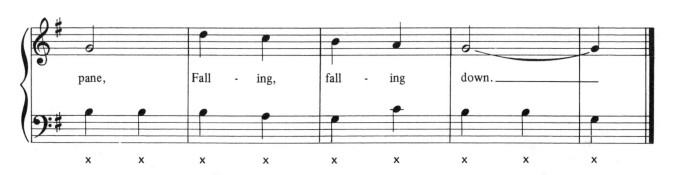

The End

Lesson 16

Jingle Bells

Briskly

Jin - gle Bells, Jin - gle Bells, Jin - gle all the

way, Oh what fun it is to ride on a

one horse o - pen sleigh. Jin - gle Bells, Jin - gle Bells,

Jin - gle all the way, Oh what fun it

is to ride on a one horse o - pen sleigh.

Lesson 16
JINGLE BELLS

1   Draw ♪♪ ♩ ♩ on the chalkboard, in large notes.

Somebody who lives at the North Pole and comes to us at Christmas has this sign on his door. Whose music sign is it?

Give several children a turn to point to the notes as they say:

Santa Claus

2   Give wrist bells to all the children.

Every day Santa has to take the sleigh and the reindeer out to get wood for the toys he is making.

While the music plays, show us how the reindeer run. When the music stops, that's the time to pile the wood on the sleigh. Then the reindeer run again.

Play:

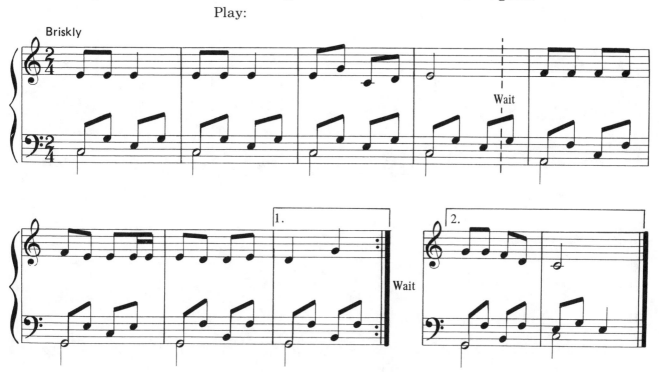

Stop to allow time for the children to "pile the wood on the sleigh."

3   **Good. This year Santa needed helpers to make special wired-up toys. First we have to saw the wood, and hammer and paint. Then we'll see how the toys work.**

Have the children saw wood, hammer, and paint in free movement.
Play Record 41-6089 S7B1 (Piano No. 10).

4   **Our first toy is a wooden soldier. Let's all see if he is a good walker.**

All the children walk as wooden soldiers.
Play Record 41-6097 S7B4 (Piano No. 31).

5   **Santa thinks a toy soldier should be able to do something besides walk forward. What do you think he can do?**

Possible responses: walk backward, walk sideways, salute with one hand slowly rising to his cap and then going down again, play an imaginary drum with two sticks (left, right, left, right) attached to his waist level in front, step in place.

Have individual children, or all of them, try out different possibilities.
Play Record 41-6097 S7B4 (Piano No. 31).

6 Here are two Raggedy Boy and Girl dolls, very floppy. We can try these out now.

All the children move like the Raggedy Boy and Girl dolls.
Play Record 41-6096 S6B3 (Piano No. 11).

7 What do you think our Raggedy Dolls can do?

Possible responses: swing their arms back and forth, sit on the floor and swing from side to side, clap their hands.
Repeat Record 41-6096 S6B3 (Piano No. 11).

8 Santa thinks all the children will like this toy—a robot. Take him walking around the room. He's made of steel, so he's pretty stiff.

Have all the children walk as robots while you play:

9 What can the robot do?

Possible responses: walk, stop, walk again; raise and lower one arm at a time; raise and lower two arms together; motion "Yes" or "No" with his head; walk in a small circle.

Play the piano or the melody line on another pitched instrument, or the drum, as for activity 8 above.

10   All the children are seated.

Fine. I think we have been good helpers for Santa.

Listen to our Christmas song. If you know it already, you can sing it with me right now.

Sing the song and teach it to the children. When the song is repeated, have a few children play finger cymbals as everyone sings.

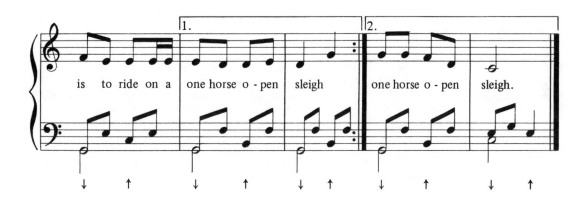

11   Obtain a baton (a stick about ¼″ round and 10″ long) used in conducting.

If we have a leader, we'll be sure to sing together.

Explain the role of the conductor in directing the singers and marking the time.

(Show.) Conduct as you sing "Jingle Bells." The conductor's beats are marked in the song. Then have all the children sing and conduct with you. Later, have one child stand in front and be the conductor (using the baton) as the other children sing and you play.

12 We can conduct the same way for other songs, too.

Encourage the children to make up their own songs in the same rhythm, or to use the melody of "Jingle Bells" with other words, conducting as they sing.

92

Example:

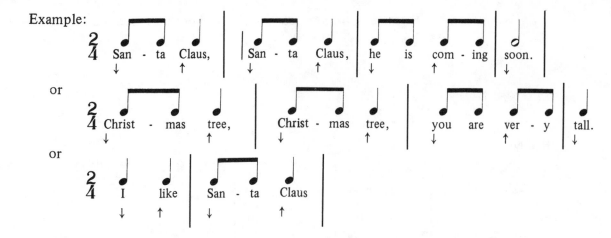

One-sentence or one-phrase songs are sufficient.

13 **Good. Now it's Christmas Eve. You can be the toy you like best, lying on the floor under the tree.**

When you hear "Jingle Bells," get up slowly and move a little to see if you are in good working order. When the song is over, lie down again under the tree.

Play very softly, as for activity 10 above.

Story Time

Characters
Santa Claus
Wooden Soldiers
Santa's Neighbors

Read the story aloud to the children. Then read it aloud again as the individual parts are carried out in movement and song by the children.

It is almost time for Santa to leave his workshop. His sleigh is full of toys.

He comes to look over the last group of wooden soldiers. He carefully winds the motor at the middle of each soldier's back.

Play the drum:

(Santa winds the motor on each soldier's back.)

Oh, what is this? The soldiers are marching backward.

Play the drum:

(The soldiers walk backward.)

Santa knows there must be a loose part somewhere. He takes his tools and turns a knob on a soldier.

Play the drum:

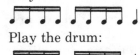

(Santa takes tools, turns a knob on a soldier.)

No, this knob is all right. He tries the knob next to it.

Play the drum:

(Santa turns another knob.)

No. This knob is all right, too. It must be the top one.

(Santa turns the top knob.)

Aha! That's it! A loose part. He fixes the loose part on each soldier.

(Santa fixes the knob on each soldier.)

Once again Santa winds the soldiers.

93

Play the drum:

Play the drum:

♩ ♩ ♩ ♩ *etc.*

Play as all the
neighbors sing and play
cymbals:

(Santa winds all the soldiers.)

Good. Now they march forward in perfect order.

(The soldiers march forward.)

Santa is happy. Everything is ready. Soon he will see his friends.

He opens the window. His Neighbors are singing as they play their cymbals.

The End

Lesson 17

The Five Little Mice

Lively

Five lit - tle mice now quick - ly go,

In - to a hole that's hid - den low. 1, 2, 3, 4,

5 they say, we're all of us home, hoo - ray! Hoo - ray!

Lesson 17
THE FIVE LITTLE MICE

1   Have all the children look at the drawings of the mice on the song page.

Let's count the mice. I don't know their names, but they're all in a story we have for today.

Have all the children point to the mice and count: 1, 2, 3, 4, 5.

See how they feel when they run around.

Have all the children run like mice.
Play Record 41-6093 S8B3 (Piano No. 22).

2   A big cat lives in the same house. Every day he practices jumping high so he can catch a mouse. The drum will tell you when he jumps.

Play the drum very slowly and softly for the cat stepping. In between the steps, at varying intervals, play a loud sound as a signal for the cat to jump.

(Children step softly)   (Jump)

Have the children step like a cat and jump once at the loud *sfz* sound.

3   Good. Sometimes, when the cat was somewhere near, only one mouse could run across the room at a time.

Number a group of children from 1 to 5. Have them stay together at one side of the room, waiting to run across in the order of their number.
Play with the drum. Vary the ways each "mouse" gets across. For example:

1st mouse—very slow, ppp ♩ ♩ ♩ *etc.*

2nd mouse—very fast, then wait, p ♫♫♩ ⁊ ⁊ ♫♫♩ *etc.*

3rd mouse—running ♫ ♫ *etc.*

4th mouse—tiptoe lightly ♪⁊ ♪⁊ ♪⁊ *etc.*

5th mouse—step, step, then run. ♩ ♩ ♫ ♫ *etc.*

Call out the number for the next one to go. A good approximation by children of the rhythm and dynamics of your drum is sufficient.

4   Here is a song the mice always sing when they get home.

Sing the song and teach it to the children.

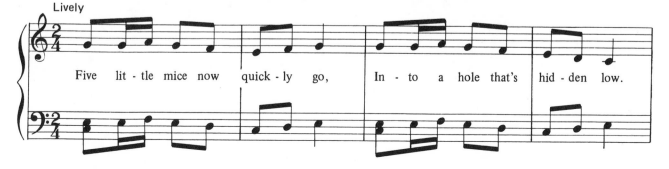

1,   2,   3,   4,   5 they   say,   we're   all   of   us home, hoo - ray! Hoo - ray!

5   **On special occasions they sing the song like this—**

Have five children in a row, squatting and facing front. Number them 1 to 5 and have them sing the song together. At "1, 2, 3, 4, 5" in the song, each child rises up at his or her number.

6   **Then the mice played the note on the piano for "home." We can do it, too.**

Give individual children a turn to play "home" on the piano (middle C, the note in front of the two black notes).

Encourage them to play and sing small phrases, such as "Now I'm home" or "I just came home." These can be played with one finger, all on the one note of C.

7   **I'll play now, while you scamper around. When you hear the music going "home," be sure to get into your hole very quickly. Make yourself small, too. Then you can come out and run again.**

Play on the piano or other pitched instrument and repeat ad lib:

Story Time

For your own sense of ease and for more effective teaching of the finger play, it is important to have it memorized—both words and gestures—beforehand.

Have the children seated near you, perhaps in a semicircle in front. Several sessions will probably be needed before the children have the play memorized and it becomes part of their repertoire.

**Up on a shelf, as you can see,
Is a really delicious piece of cheese,
And five little mice, each with his share,
Are eating away without a care.**

**A cat is prowling 'round the house,
He jumps up high to catch a mouse,
The mice are faster and down they go,
Into a hole that's hidden low.**

**1, 2, 3, 4, 5, they say,
We're all of us home, Hooray! Hooray!**

On special occasions the five mice sing:

Play on the piano or other pitched instrument as all sing.

Lively

Five lit-tle mice now quick-ly go, In-to a hole that's hid-den low.

1, 2, 3, 4, 5 they say, we're all of us home, hoo-ray! Hoo-ray!

The End

Lesson 18

Let's Go to the Circus

The cir - cus is in town, They're march - ing down the street, let's go, let's go, let's go, let's go, let's go, let's go.

Lesson 18
LET'S GO TO THE CIRCUS

1 **I saw a big sign today. It said, "The Circus Is Coming to Town."**

> Show as many circus pictures as you can and ask for contributions to discussion from those children who have been to the circus or have seen one on TV.
>
> Talk with the children about the clowns, the trapeze performers, the bareback riders, the trained animals, the band, and the popcorn stands.

Suppose we are the circus people. The first thing we must have is a parade through the town, so everyone will know we're here.

We have a really peppy song while we're marching. Listen—

> Sing the song and teach it to the children.

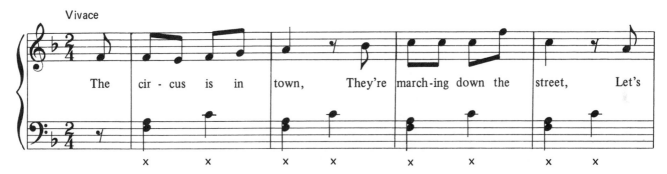

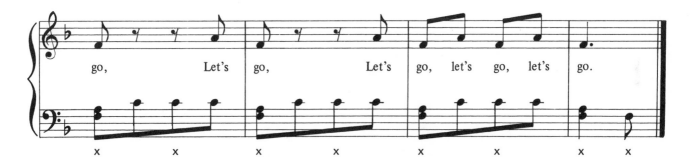

2 Have a small drum and three or four tambourines.

The drum beats all the way through the song, while everyone is marching. Then the tambourines join in when we sing, "Let's go, let's go, let's go, let's go, let's go."

> Have the children make up a circus parade. The drummer carries the drum as he or she plays (marked *x* in the song.) The tambourine players also march, shaking the tambourines at "Let's go," etc., to the end of the song.
>
> Encourage the children to walk "in character." The clowns wave to the people watching along the streets, the elephant walks swinging his trunk, the ringmaster might swing a whip above his or her head once in a while.
>
> Play the song as for activity 1 above on the piano or another pitched instrument as the children march and sing. It can be repeated once or twice as the children continue to march and sing.

You can play the following measures as a bridge between repetitions:

(The)

3   Now we're back at the circus grounds. It's time for the elephants to practice their act.

The wonderful thing about these elephants is that they can count.

> The children stand as elephants, hands clasped in front for a trunk, bent over a little.
>
> Play two, three, or four beats on the drum while the children stamp one foot the number of beats played.

4

> Obtain a short rope to serve as a ringmaster's whip.

Good. Now the lions are waiting to practice, too. When the ringmaster cracks the whip, they all stand up and roar. When he cracks his whip again, they go down.

> The children get down on their hands and knees in a circle as "lions." Ask one child to stand at the center as the ringmaster. Having the lions come up a few times with a very short period to "roar" is better than a long "roaring" time.

5   Those are good lions. Everyone will like them. The trapeze people come up now to swing and jump.

> Have the children swing their arms at their sides, up and back, in a slight down and up movement with supple knees (as in pumping a swing), till they jump forward with both feet together. As they swing, you can say "Swing, swing, swing, swing, swing, *jump*."
>
> Repeat several times.

6   Here is the music for the galloping horses and the bareback riders.

> The children gallop, some with arms outstretched as though standing on the horse.
>
> Play Record 41-6097 S8B3 (Piano No. 14).

7   Good. Now we'll have clown practice.

> Have the children stand in a place on the floor with sufficient space around them to move freely. Ask them to take different clown poses, holding each one until you call "Change" with one sharp drum beat.
>
> Encourage poses that are varied, such as on the floor with one foot in the air, bending over and looking through the legs, or standing with arms and legs very outstretched.
>
> Watch to see that no pose is taken that is not stable enough to be held until you call "Change."

8   Now we have the new—never seen before—Rocket Man!

> (A rocket man is propelled from a device that looks like a rocket.)
>
> Have one child be the Rocket Man. He or she stands and waits to jump at the sound of "Blastoff!" Have everyone else chant as you play the drum:

"5, 4, 3, 2, 1, Blastoff!"

Give other children a chance to be the Rocket Man.

9   The last to practice are the acrobats.

> Have the children do anything in free movement that suggests acrobats to them—stretches, swings with a partner, or somersaults.
> Play Record 41-6091 S4B3 (Piano No. 18).

10   Popcorn, ice cream, sugar cones—there are always a lot of good things to eat at the circus. What could we sell?

> Give individual children a turn to walk around, playing the triangle and calling out their choice of something to sell.

11   When the circus is over, many people buy pennants as a remembrance. A picture of the elephant that can count is on each one.
As they walk home, they sing and wave the flags in time with the song.

> Play the song as in activity 1 above. The children walk and sing, some waving imaginary flags.

Story Time

> Read the story aloud. Then read it aloud again as the individual parts are carried out in movement and song by the children. One or more children can take an individual part.

Characters
Circus Band and
  Singers
Benjy
Benjy's Friends
The Circus Man

Play on the piano or
other pitched
instrument:

The signs had been up for weeks: "The Circus Is Coming to Town!" Now the band was actually marching down Main Street! Some of the circus people sang, too.

(The Circus Band sings and marches.)

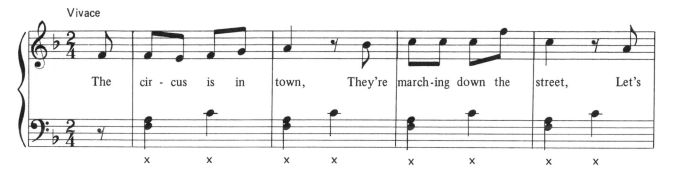

(Benjy and his Friends follow the parade.)

How exciting it was for Benjy and his friends to watch! They followed the parade all the way to the tent grounds.

A sign was posted on one of the tents: "Clowns wanted. Apply within." "Oh," said Benjy, "would I like that job!"

Benjy and his friends went into the tent. The man inside said, "Well, I'll give you a tryout. Let's see how many clown poses you can do, a different one every time there's a drum beat with the word 'Change.'"

Benjy and his friends moved into an open space. They took a clown pose as the drum played ♩.
sfz

Play one strong beat on the drum (♩).
sfz

(Benjy and his Friends take a clown pose.)

Play drum as above and say *"Change,"* ♩.
sfz

(They change.)

Play drum as above.

(They change again.)

Now the drum beats came faster.

As above, four drum beats with just enough time for everyone to change the pose. Say "Change" with the drum beat.

Pose (hold)   Pose (hold)   Pose (hold)   Pose (hold)

(They change with each fast beat.)

"That's really good," said the man. "You can have the job." So Benjy and his friends worked as clowns all the time the circus was in town.

The circus man said the people had never laughed so much.

The End

Lesson 19

The Caterpillar

Moderato

Cat - er - pil - lar, Cat - er - pil - lar, Wait and see,

You will be a but - ter - fly, High in the sky.

Lesson 19
THE CATERPILLAR

1   Obtain pictures of butterflies for the children to see, showing the great variety of butterflies, their beautiful colors, and the lightness of their wings.

Butterflies like to go where there are many flowers. Who would like to be a flower? You can be a rose, a daisy, a goldenrod, or any flower you wish.

          Have several children stand like flowers in the room.

Now everyone else can fly like a butterfly. Sometimes the butterfly stays near a flower and moves its wings softly up and down until it flies again.

          Play Record 41-6097 S7B2 (Piano No. 20).

2   Have pictures of caterpillars to show the children. Tell how the butterfly was first a caterpillar.

In the summertime, if we looked hard, we might see a caterpillar in the grass. Let's crawl on the floor and we can find out how he feels as he moves along. You can nibble on a blade of grass once in a while, too.

          The children move freely.
          Play the drum if you wish, softly and irregularly, for accompaniment:

3   **Good. Now, when it's time for the caterpillar to change into a butterfly, he makes a little house out of twigs and grass and goes inside. The little house is called a cocoon.**
    Make your little house. Then go inside and be very, very still while you're changing into a butterfly.

          Have all the children gather twigs and grass to make their cocoons in free movement and then roll themselves into a ball on the floor.

4   **Ssh ... ssh.**

          All the children are very still for an appropriate time.

    When we hear the butterfly music, we know we've changed into butterflies. It's time to open the door and come out. Then we can fly away.

          Play Record 41-6097 S7B2 (Piano No. 20).

5   **We have a song to sing to the caterpillar. We want him to know that he's going to change into a butterfly.**

          Sing the song and teach it to the children.

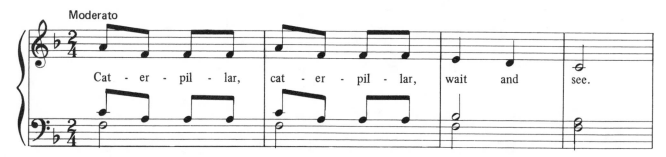

You will be a but-ter-fly, high in the sky.

6   Draw this on the chalkboard:

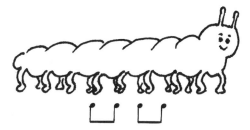

This caterpillar is so long that it needs two sets of running notes to say its name.

> Give individual children turns to point to the notes as they say "ca-ter-pil-lar."

7   Maybe the caterpillar will be sure to wait if we play a drum when we sing "wait and see." Like this—

> Sing the song, adding the drum beat to "wait and see."
> Give individual children a turn to play the drum as everyone else sings.
> (It is possible to sing only the first phrase of the song for this.)

8   Draw ♩ ♩ 𝅝 on the chalkboard.

These are the music signs for "wait and see."

> Call attention to how different they look from ♪♩ ♪♩ for "caterpillar."

When I call your name, go to the board and choose either the caterpillar sign or the "wait and see" sign. Point to it, and tell us which one it is.

> Give individual children a turn.

9   Now my chalk is telling the story, too. Here's the caterpillar—

> Draw a long, relatively straight line as you sing:
>
> "Caterpillar, caterpillar"
>
> Draw: _____

Here's the butterfly going up:

> Sing: "You will be a butterfly"

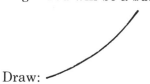

> Draw:

(Benjy), will you draw for the caterpillar as you sing? (Amy), you can draw for the butterfly and sing, too.

For your own sense of ease, and for more effective teaching of the finger play, it is important to have it memorized—both words and gestures—beforehand.

Have the children seated near you, perhaps in a semicircle in front. Several sessions will probably be needed before the children have the play memorized and it becomes part of their repertoire.

Note: The second verse can be omitted for very young children.

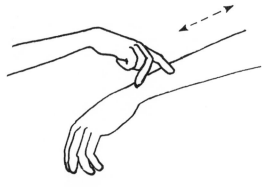

**Here's a little caterpillar,
Yellow and round,
He goes very slowly,
Down on the ground.**

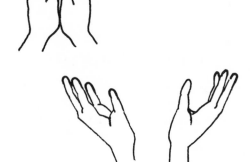

**He makes a little house,
It's called a cocoon,
Then he opens the door,
Not a minute too soon.**

**Now he's a butterfly,
Up he goes high,
Shining his wings,
All day in the sky.**

Lesson 20

To Johnny's House

Moderato

I'm on my way to John - ny's house, Oh

which way to go, Oh which way to go?

Lesson 20
TO JOHNNY'S HOUSE

1   Johnny has a new house. We have to find out how to get there. We even have a song about it.

We'll learn the song, so we can sing it while we're walking on the way.

Sing the song and teach it to the children.

I'm on my way to John-ny's house, oh which way to go? Oh which way to go?

2   **Good. We might have to try different roads to find Johnny's house. (Benjy), will you show us where one road might go?**

Give a starting point to one child. He walks in any direction as everyone sings the song. He walks until the song is ended.

3   **(Amy), you can show us another road. Start from the same place (Benjy) did.**

(Amy) also walks, but in a different direction from the road taken by (Benjy). Again, everyone sings the song, and (Amy) walks until the song is ended.

Give one or two other children a turn to choose a different road.

4   The children are seated. Draw a large map on the chalkboard like the one shown. Have a card-sized version of the map for the child.

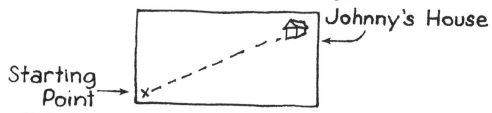

This is a picture called a map.

Tell the children how the map shows the road that goes to Johnny's house. Relate the outline of the map to the room boundaries, showing the starting point and Johnny's house.

(Benjy), this is a map just like the one on the board. Take it and walk on the road it shows to Johnny's house. Then come back again.

You can walk slowly or, if you're in a hurry, you can walk quickly. When you come back, go to the board and draw a line right next to the road you went on.

Give other children the chance to do the same. They can choose their own ways to go—slow or fast, skipping, or walking.

5   Draw a different map on the board, like the one shown. Have a card-sized version of the map for the child.

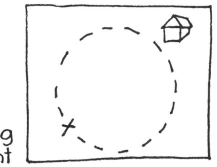

Johnny's House

Starting Point

If you had a friend with an airplane, he might take you for a ride past Johnny's house and back home again.

> Show the children how the airplane is going in a circle past Johnny's house and back again.

(Benjy), will you take this map and show us the way the airplane went? When you come back, go to the board and draw a line on the map right next to the way you went.

> Repeat the starting point in the room, and where it is shown on the map. Give other children a turn to do the same.

6   Good. Now, here are our two maps. One is a road map and one is an airplane map.
(Benjy), choose one card and show us if you are following the road or flying in a circle in the airplane.

> Have other children take a turn to choose a card and carry out its direction. They can move in any tempo or rhythm they wish.

7   The children are seated around the piano or other pitched instrument.

Johnny is going to have a party at his new house. Let's play all the good things there might be to eat. We'll play on middle C.

> Show middle C, the key in front of the two black notes.

I'll start with apples.   Play C C.

> Give as many children as possible a turn. All responses are good—ice cream, peaches, strawberry cake, or an orange.

8   Write the end phrases of the song on the chalkboard, like this:

Let's sing this part of our new song again. These are the music signs for "Oh, which way to go, oh, which way to go?" I'll point to the signs as we sing.

> All the children sing the song with you. Point to the notes for "Oh, which way to go, oh, which way to go?"

9   You can hear that we sing "Oh, which way to go?" two times. (Benjy), will you come and point to the way that goes up? Sing it, too.

> Give other children a turn to point to the way that goes down or up. Have each child sing.

10 Now I'm making a ladder on the piano to get to the note that sings "Oh."

> Demonstrate, starting on middle C, singing 1, 2, 3, 4, 5. Number 5 is "Oh." Then you can go either way, like this:

Play and sing—1, 2, 3, 4, 5
Then play—5   5   6   7 8
and sing—"Oh, which way to go?"

or you can go like this:

Play and sing—1, 2, 3, 4, 5
Then play—5   4   3   2 1
and sing—"Oh, which way to go?"

Give as many children as possible a turn to play and sing one or the other, one ending high and one ending low.

11   There will be a party at Johnny's new house, and everyone will sing the songs they know. Take a partner and swing while I play a song we like. As soon as you know which one it is, sing it too while you swing. I might play the song two times, maybe even three times.

When the song changes, take a different partner.

Play the songs that are best known, such as "I'm Going Up," "The Farmer in the Dell," and "High-Stepping Horses." Two or three songs played three times each are sufficient.

In repeating a song, you might vary it by playing the melody alone or changing the dynamics by playing it very softly.

Story Time

Characters
Johnny
Johnny's Mother
Benjy
Amy
Josh
Johnny's Friends

("Map" on board)

(Small map to carry)

Play the drum:

Play the drum:

Play as all sing "To Johnny's House."

Read the story aloud to the children. Then read it aloud again as the individual parts are carried out in movement and song by the children. One or any number of children can take an individual part.

Johnny had just moved to a new house. Now he was mailing out invitations to a party. All his friends would come. Johnny's mother said, "Why don't you send a map to your friends so they will know how to get here?

"That's a good idea," answered Johnny. He made a map that he sent to everyone.

Benjy and Amy went to the party together. Before they started, they looked at the map on the wall and went over the road they should take in chalk.

(Benjy and Amy draw a line on the wall map.)

On the way, they also looked at the small map they carried, to be sure they were going in the right direction.

(They look at the small map they are carrying.)

Johnny was happy to see his friends. "I am glad you could follow a map," he said. Just then they heard an airplane buzzing in the sky. Everyone went outside to look. "That's Josh," they all shouted.

The plane made a circle, right past the new house.

(Josh runs in a circle, like an "airplane.")

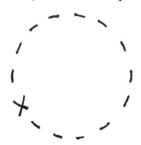

Everyone had a wonderful time at the party. At the end they sang about going to Johnny's house.

Moderato

I'm on my way to John-ny's house, oh which way to go? Oh which way to go?

The End

Lesson 21

Boo!

Step Step   Step Step   Ooooo - ooh BOO!
(Clap)

Lesson 21
BOO!

1 **Halloween is next week. What are some of the things we'll need?**

>Probable responses: witches, ghosts, a full moon, black cats, dark shadows, a haunted house in a dark forest, waving tree branches, a pot for brewing charms, snails, snakes, or tiger tails.

We'll try the witches on a broomstick first. Hold tightly to your broomstick as you go through the sky.

>Play Record 41-6097 S8B3 (Piano No. 14.)

2 The children are seated on the floor.

Let's sit around our magic pot and stir the witches' brew. We'll see what comes out of the pot.

>(Show.) Stir the brew as you say softly and mysteriously any rhyming syllables, such as:
>
>POUT
>MOUT
>
>Now it comes OUT! A GHOST!
>
>Give as many children as possible a turn to make their own chant as they stir the brew and tell what came out.
>
>Any syllables are good. Any object related to Halloween can come out of the brew—a black cat, a monster, a black spider, or costumed characters such as a clown or a gypsy.

3 **Now (Benjy) can work his magic on a drum, and we'll all turn into what he makes.**

>(Benjy) beats the drum softly, then calls out his choice.
>
>*Example:* Drum ♩ ♩ ♩ ♩ *Cats*
>
>All the children now move like cats. You can accompany their movement with a drum, playing softly: ♩ ♩ for slow cats. ♩♪ for galloping witches, or possibly ♫ ♫ (slow) for a ghost.
>
>Give other children a turn to play the drum and say what came out. A very short time for each Halloween character is best. All should be done in free movement.

4 The children are seated. They have rhythm sticks.

This is ghost practice. Play very softly with me till you hear a *loud* beat. That's the ghost's "BOO." Play the same loud beat *right* after.

>Play on the drum very softly, till the very loud beat, like this:

Softly ♩ ♩ ♩ ♩ ♩
sf

Children ♩ ♩ ♩ ♩ ♩
sf

>Repeat as many times as desirable. Vary the length of the soft beats to make the *sfz* beat a surprise.

5 **Good. Now you can be the ghost stepping very softly. When you hear the same loud sound, call out "BOO" and raise your arms. Make sure it's the kind of "BOO" that will really scare somebody.**

>Play the drum with very soft beats, as the children step like ghosts. At unexpected times, play the loud *sfz* beat.

6

The children are seated around the piano or another pitched instrument.

That was good. I think you make very fine ghosts.

You will see that the piano is especially good for ghosts that tiptoe and say "BOO."
Listen—

On the piano play single notes, very soft and short, on any notes till, with both hands outstretched, you play down anywhere to make the loud "BOO."

On xylophone or bells, one stick playing the soft notes and both sticks together playing the "BOO" will create a similar effect.

Give as many children as possible a turn.

7   Listen to the ghost's song—

Sing the song and teach it to the children.

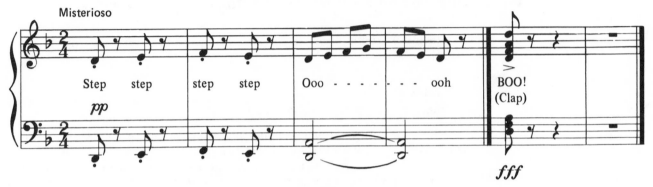

Have the children hold their hands close together in preparation for the last loud clap with "BOO!"

8

Put the music notes for "Oooh" on the board.

Here are the music signs for "Oooh—oooh"

Show how "Oooh—oooh" can be sung going up 1, 2, 3, 4, and down 3, 2, 1.
Sing several times with the children, using the numbers.

9   If I start on the note right next to middle C, I can play the ghost's song on the piano.
Like this—

(Show.) Middle C—in front of the two black notes, with D next door.
Play and sing the numbers:

D   E   F   G   F   E   D
1   2   3   4   3   2   1

Give the children turns to play, with one finger if that is easiest. Help them to start if necessary. (The same applies with a xylophone or bells.)

10 Now it's Halloween. There's a full moon in the sky, but it's pretty dark anyway.
Listen to what happens.

All the children can move as they choose, like cats, ghosts, or witches. When you call a name, the individual child makes a sound related to Halloween, like "oooooooh," or "rrrrrrrrrrr," or "m-e-o-w."
Play (softly) Record 41-6086 S1B1 (Piano No. 25.)

Story Time

Read the story aloud to the children. Then read it aloud again as the individual parts are carried out in movement and in song by the children.

Characters
Boo the Ghost
Benjy
Little Girl
Little Boy
Benjy's Friends

Play the drum:

etc.

Play the drum:

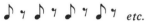

etc.

Play the drum:

♩ ♩ ♩ ♩ etc.

Play the drum softly:

♪ ⁊ ♪ ⁊ ♪ ⁊ ♪ ⁊ etc.

Play the drum:

etc.

Play the drum softly:

♪ ⁊ ♪ ⁊ ♪ ⁊ ♪ ⁊ etc.

Play the drum:

etc.

Play as all sing and clap on BOO!

Once upon a time there was a ghost named Boo. He was named Boo because his favorite game was to tiptoe behind someone and shout "Boo!" Of course, Halloween was his special holiday.

One Halloween, Benjy was in the park. He saw a little girl gathering autumn leaves.

(The Little Girl gathers leaves.)

Suddenly Boo appeared behind her. He shouted, "Boo!"

(Boo shouts behind Little Girl.)

"Oh, oh," cried out the little girl as she dropped her leaves and ran quickly away.

(The Little Girl drops her leaves and runs away.)

Boo laughed. Now Benjy saw what happened next. A little boy was bouncing his ball.)

(The Little Boy bounces his ball.)

Here came Boo again, to tiptoe up behind the little boy.

(Boo tiptoes up behind the Little Boy)

Then he shouted, "Boo!"

(Boo shouts.)

The little boy left his ball and ran off as fast as he could.

(The Little Boy runs off.)

How Boo laughed! "I know what to do," thought Benjy. He waited until Boo was looking around for someone else to scare. Now Benjy crept up softly behind him.

(Benjy creeps up softly behind Boo.)

Then he shouted, "BOO!"

Boo jumped so high that he nearly jumped out of his white robe, and he ran so fast and so far that he was never seen again.

(Boo jumps high and runs off.)

Now every Halloween Benjy and his friends sing a special song to remember Boo and his tricks.

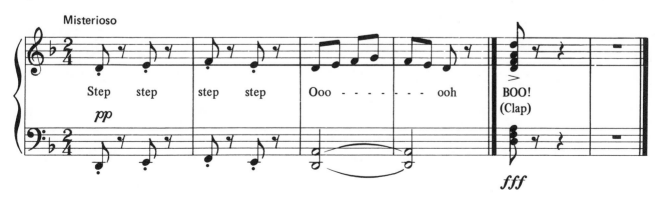

The End

I Love You
(Valentine's Day)

I'm send-ing you a Val-en-tine, It says that I love you.___

Tra la la la, la la la la, Tra la la la la la la la la.___

116

Lesson 22
I LOVE YOU
(Valentine's Day)

1   Show a Valentine's Day card to the children.

See what the postman brought me this morning! It's a valentine, to say "You are my good friend and I love you."

Once there was a man named Valentine who loved many people, so now we have a Valentine's Day to think of everyone we love.

I think this valentine is made of strong cardboard. Make a picture with your arms, and let's see how this valentine would walk.

                               (Play Record 41-6091 S3B4 (Piano No. 16).

2   **Good. I think that valentine might say, "Daddy dear, Mommy dear, I love you."**

(Benjy), will you play "I love you" on the xylophone? Play it strongly, like the strong cardboard valentine. Sing while you play, too.

                               Give individual children a turn to play "I love you" on the xylophone (strongly) as they sing.

3   **Now we need a very special valentine for a friend, a very pretty valentine. What would we use to make it?**

                               Possible responses: tissue paper, lace, pink ribbon, flowers.

This is a very soft and gentle valentine. Close your eyes for a minute and maybe you can see a beautiful, sweet valentine.

                               Have the children sit on the floor, or stand, and move only their arms as the very gentle valentine.

                               Play Record 41-6096 S6B3 (Piano No. 11).

4   **(Amy), will you take the triangle and play "I love you" as softly and sweetly as your valentine would say it? Sing it, too.**

                               Give individual children a turn to play the soft and gentle "I love you" on the triangle as they sing.

5   **Fine. Now, if we make a valentine that's very, very strong, even stronger than strong cardboard, we might stand it in the park, like a statue. What would we use to make it?**

                               Possible responses: steel, wood, iron, stone.

                               Have the children take any pose as the very strongest valentine. (Encourage varied poses, such as kneeling on one knee, in a half-reclining position, or in a sitting position, as well as those done in a standing position.)

                               Go around to each child, feeling an arm or a leg to see if they are "strong enough."

6   **(Janie), please go and play "I love you" on the drum for this very strong valentine.**

                               Give individual children a turn to play a very strong "I love you" on the drum as they sing.

7   Have the children get into a circle. Place four note cards on a table (♩, ♩, ♫, ♩ ♪) along with one large valentine envelope.

Now we can take our valentines to our friends. When it's your turn, pick the card that tells which way you want to go.

Have one child pick a card from the table, show the card to everyone, place the card in the envelope, and take the envelope around the circle along with the rhythm of the card.

Play the drum in the same rhythm.

When you stop the drum, the child also stops and gives the envelope to the child beside him or her. The children then change places and the child with the envelope now picks his or her own rhythm card.

Repeat until as many children as possible have had turns to carry the envelope.

8 Every year, when Valentine's Day comes, we can sing this song. Listen—

Sing the song and teach it to the children.

9 I like to hear the song this way. Tell me if you do, too.

Have one child stand in front and sing the first part of the song and the other children join in with the chorus of "Tra la la la" etc.

Give several children a turn to be the soloist.

10 This is a good song for a partner dance.

Have the children take partners, face each other, join hands, and swing from side to side as they sing:

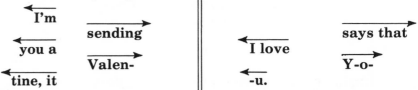

At "Tra la," have them drop hands and skip around each other in the same place, skipping and singing the chorus until the end of the song.

Repeat the song as the children take hands to sing and swing with the first part of the song, then sing and skip around their partners at the chorus.

Play as for activity 8 above. (For very young children, the gallop can be substituted for the skip.)

Story Time

Read the story aloud. Then read it aloud again as the individual parts are carried out in movement and song by the children.

Characters
Benjy
The Pink Valentine
The Wood Valentine
The Dancing Valentine
The Friends of the
    Dancing Valentine
(A triangle)
(A drum)

Valentine, Valentine, on the wall,
Who is the fairest of them all?

Soon it would be Valentine's Day. The walls of the little shop were covered with valentines. And all of them were different.

Benjy wondered which one to choose. As he looked and looked, a pretty Pink Valentine made of tissue paper and lace stepped out and sang softly while it played on the triangle: "I love you."

(The Pink Valentine steps out and plays "I love you" on the triangle.)

Benjy was just about to say, "Oh, I choose you!" when another valentine appeared. This one was made of wood. It sang strongly and played on the drum: "I love you."

(The Wood Valentine steps out and plays "I love you" on drum.)

Benjy liked the Wood Valentine, too. But now a Dancing Valentine tiptoed into the room. She brought many Friends with her. They took hands and swung their arms as they sang, and then skipped with the chorus of the song.

(A Dancing Valentine and her Friends tiptoed in to sing and dance.)

Play the piano or another pitched instrument as the Dancing Valentine and her Friends sing and dance.

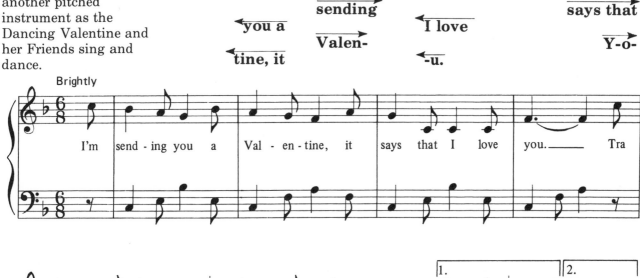

"That was very beautiful," said Benjy.
I never did find out which one he took. Which one do *you* think?

The End

Lesson 23

The Sleep Fairy
and Her Lullaby

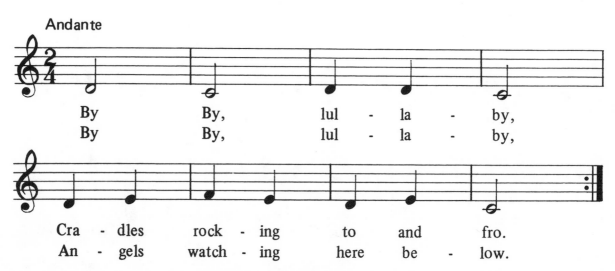

Andante

By   By,   lul - la - by,
By   By,   lul - la - by,

Cra - dles   rock - ing   to   and   fro.
An - gels   watch - ing   here   be - low.

Lesson 23
THE SLEEP FAIRY AND HER LULLABY

1   Let's have a good game of practice tag. I'll play the drum while you run. When the drum beat stops, you stop too, and touch the person next to you. Be sure it's a very light touch.

Then we start all over again, going in the opposite direction.

Play running notes (♪♪) on the drum in phrases of irregular length—long, short, very short, long, and so on.

2   That was fun. Now I want you to listen for high sounds and low sounds. When I play high, raise your arms and make your hands twinkle very fast like the stars at night.

When I play low, kneel down and tap on the floor.

Play on the piano or other pitched instrument:

Alternate: A-B, A-A, A-B, B-B.

3

You can wear the wrist bells for a really good skip. I'll play big skips that take you up high and little soft skips that stay close to the ground. Maybe you are skipping on the path in a beautiful park.

Play the drum, alternating between very strong and very soft.

(High Skips)

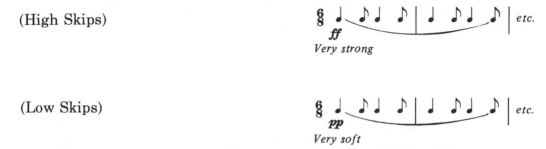

(Low Skips)

4   Now we come inside the house. How quiet it is! Let's listen together. What do we hear?

Possible responses: a clock ticking, someone moving, footsteps outside the room, an auto horn from the street outside, a distant church bell, the hum of traffic.

Several short periods of listening in absolute silence, telling "what was heard" in between, are usually better than one longer period.

5   It's almost as quiet as "go to sleep" time. If you had a new puppy, how would you rock it to sleep?

Give individual children a turn to "rock the puppy to sleep," either swinging their arms while holding the puppy or swinging with a whole body swing from side to side (seated).

6   The puppy would go to sleep faster if you sang to it. Listen—

Sing the song and teach it to the children. Swing from side to side as you sing. (The children swing also, still seated.)

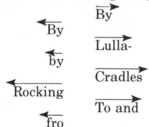

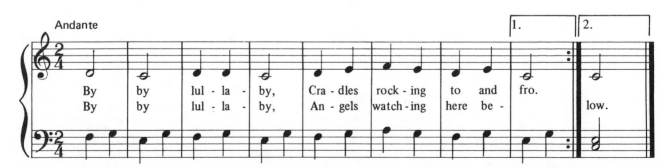

7   This time, instead of singing the words, I'll make a humming sound. Let's all try it. Keep your lips closed and make the sound of "mmmmm" way up high inside your mouth.

Play the song very softly on the piano or another pitched instrument, and hum with the children.

Swing as for activity 6 above, if desired.

8   We know other things that rock. This is a rocking horse that goes forward and back.

(Show.) Standing, with one foot forward, go forward and back.

Then hum the song with the children as they go forward and back with you.

By	(forward)
By	(back)
Lulla-	(forward)
By	(back)

9   A little boat rocks on the waves, too.

Have the children take partners and sit on the floor facing each other, with knees bent and feet touching. Have them join hands and rock back and forth, again as everyone hums (as in activity 8).

10

The children are seated.

Sometimes you might have a little puppy or a kitten—maybe a doll—that needs to be rocked to sleep. (Benjy), will you show us a lullaby you might sing?

Encourage any short phrases, such as "Go to sleep my dolly dear," as the child rocks the "doll" or "Puppy, puppy, go to sleep" or just "Sleep, sleep, sleep, sleep," with the rocking movement.

If desirable, everyone can repeat an individual lullaby. Any effort is valuable, regardless of accuracy of pitch or rhythm.

11

Give the children rhythm sticks.

Just before we go to sleep at night, we often look at our picture books. My book has a picture of rhythm stick players in a band.

I'll play a marching song now. You can be the rhythm stick players and play with me.

Have the children play with you as you play on the piano or other pitched instrument:

"Yankee Doodle"

12   The Three Bears might be in the picture book, too. How did Papa Bear say, "Who's been eating from *my* bowl?"

Most of the children will answer with "Who's been eating from *my* bowl?" in a deep, strong voice.

How did Mama Bear say, "Who's been eating from *my* bowl?

Most of the children will reply in the appropriate voice of Mama Bear.

And what did Baby Bear say?

Most of the children will answer in the high voice of Baby Bear.

13 Now it's time for the sleep fairies to fly around and look in at all the houses. They want to see if everyone is tucked in and asleep. I think they fly very softly.

You can be a sleep fairy now. When the music stops, come and sit down near me.

Play Record 41-6088 S5B3 (Piano No. 1).

Story Time

Characters
The Sleep Fairy
Fairy Helpers
The Three Bears:
    Papa Bear
    Mama Bear
    Baby Bear
Benjy

Read the story aloud. Then read it aloud again as the individual parts are carried out in movement and song by the children.

The Sleep Fairy didn't know what to do! Benjy's sleep time was long past and he was still awake.

"I'll play some marching music for him," she thought. She called her Fairy Helpers, and they came and played the rhythm sticks with "Yankee Doodle."

(The Fairy Helpers play rhythm sticks with "Yankee Doodle.")

Play on the piano or other pitched instrument:

It was a good marching piece, loud and peppy. Benjy liked it, but he did not go to sleep.

"Oh, dear," said the Sleep Fairy. "I'll show him his favorite book people." And she brought out the Three Bears.

(The Sleep Fairy brings out the Three Bears.)

Papa Bear said, "Who's been eating from *my* bowl?"

(Papa Bear speaks.)

Mama Bear said, "Who's been eating from *my* bowl?"

(Mama Bear speaks.)

Baby Bear said, "Who's been eating from *my* bowl, and ate it all up?"

(Baby Bear speaks.)

Benjy liked that, too, but he did not go to sleep. Then the Sleep Fairy said, "I know. We'll sing him a lullaby." Again she called her Fairy Helpers.

(The Fairy Helpers come in.)

They swung from side to side as they hummed like this, very softly and gently—

(The fairy helpers swing and hum.)

Play the piano or other pitched instrument as the fairy helpers sing.

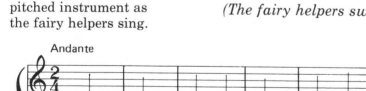

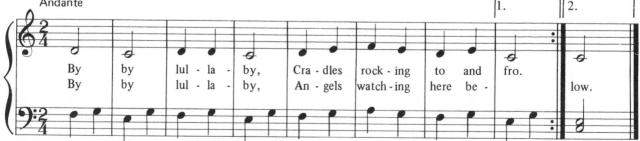

Benjy's eyes began to close. As the lullaby ended, he was sound asleep.

The End

A Needle and Thread

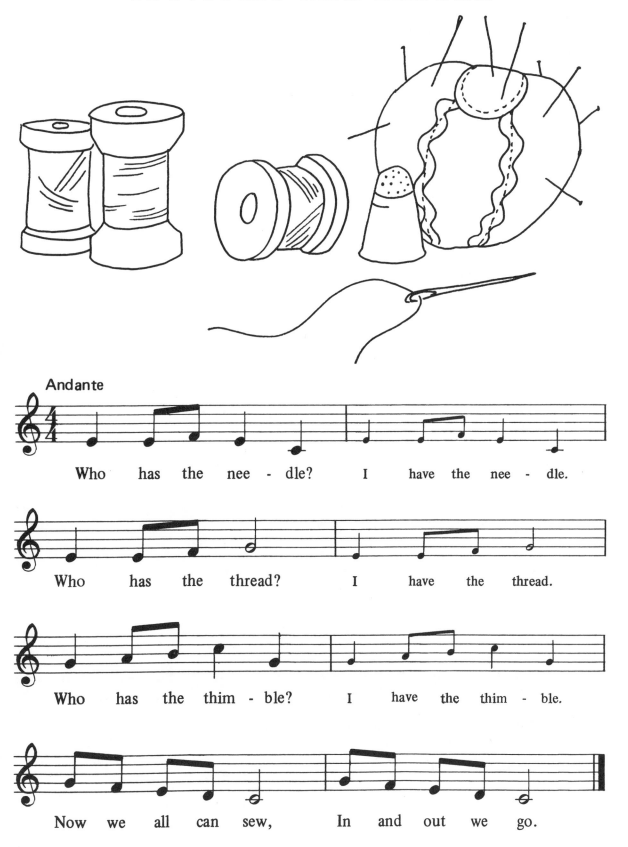

Andante

Who has the nee - dle? I have the nee - dle.

Who has the thread? I have the thread.

Who has the thim - ble? I have the thim - ble.

Now we all can sew, In and out we go.

Lesson 24
A NEEDLE AND THREAD

1   Let's walk along with a song we know. Today we'll do it this way.

    Have one child walk as he sings a song that everyone knows, such as "High-Stepping Horses," or "Oh, Do You Know the Muffin Man?" Then have everyone repeat the song, also walking as they sing.

    Play the piano or another pitched instrument when the song repeats. (The children can walk in a circle or separately.)

    Do two or three songs in the same way, with different children to sing and step alone first.

2   The children are seated. Give them all rhythm sticks.

Good. Now we'll play together in a special way. Whatever I do, you do after me. Be sure to wait while I'm playing.

    Play a short phrase on the drum like one of those below. Then have the children echo the phrase by playing the rhythm sticks. (One phrase may be repeated several times if desired.)

    To encourage the children to start their response together, you can say "Go" on the last beat of the drum phrase. The "Go" will serve as an anacrusis or preparation for the children's echo of your phrase.

3   Everybody stand up, and we'll do the same thing in another way. I'll play the drum and you can step what I played.

    As in activity 2 above, play a short phrase on the drum, like one of the phrases below. Then have the children step to the same rhythm. (One phrase may be repeated several times if desired.)

    You can say "Go" on the last beat of the drum beat as in activity 2. A good general response is sufficient.

4   Now we'll do some clown poses, with one clown to start and everybody to follow.

    One child stands in front and takes a clown pose as you play one strong beat on the drum and call "Pose." Then call "Everybody" and play two strong beats on the drum as the other children imitate the pose held by the first child.

    Again, play a strong beat on the drum and call "Change" as the child in front takes a different pose. Again, call "Everybody" and play two strong beats on the drum as the other children imitate the new pose.

    Four or five poses are sufficient for one child to initiate. Several children might have turns to be in front.

5 We'll do that again some time soon. Here is a song we all know. Let's sing it this way. I'll sing a part with "la" and you do the same after me.

Sing (and play on the piano or other pitched instrument if you wish) the first verse of a song known to the children, such as "I'm Going Up" (from Lesson 2), singing "la."

The children sing the same. Now sing the second part of the song with "la." The children sing the same.

6 Let's do the same thing with another song we know. First listen and tell me which one it is.

Sing (and play on the piano or other pitched instrument if you wish) the song "Rain" (from Lesson 6, activity 1), singing with "la."

Now sing the first phrase with "la." The children sing the same after you.

Sing the second phrase with "la." The children sing the same after you.

Sing the third phrase with "la." The children sing the same after you.

7 A needle, a thimble, and a spool of thread are needed for this game activity. (A large darning needle can be mounted on a piece of cardboard and covered with Scotch tape.)

The children are seated in a circle.

This is a new guessing game for us to sing and play.

Sing the song as you carry out the game in a "practice time," like this:

The children close their eyes. Place the needle, the thread, and the thimble in the hands of three children.

The children open their eyes and the question and answer song begins. You sing, "Who has the needle?"

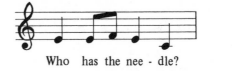

Who has the nee - dle?

The child who has the needle holds it up and sings, "I have the needle."

I have the nee - dle.

You sing, "Who has the thread?"

The child who has the thread sings, "I have the thread."

You sing, "Who has the thimble?"

The child who has the thimble sings, "I have the thimble."

Everyone sings as they make the gesture in the air of sewing in and out: "In and out we go, that is how we sew."

Repeat the game with different children being given the three objects. (Some children may need to have the use of the thimble explained to them.)

8 We can even sing the song without playing the game.

Play the piano or another pitched instrument and sing with the children as everyone sings all parts of the song.

9 Now we'll sing it again another way.

>Divide the children, with one half to sing the question, the other half to sing the answer, and everyone together for "This is how we sew, in and out we go."
>Reverse the parts and repeat the song if desirable.
>Play as for activity 8 above.

10 This time, sing with "la" instead of the words.

>Have the children sing either the question or the answer as in activity 9, but with "la" instead of the words.
>Play as for activity 8.
>Reverse the parts and repeat the song if desired.

Story Time

Read the story aloud. Then read it aloud again as the individual parts are carried out in movement and song by the children. Any number of children can take an individual part.

Characters
Benjy
The Parrot
The Neighbors

Once upon a time when Benjy was in the pet shop, he saw a beautiful green Parrot. Now, you know that parrots can imitate sounds and words.

So when Benjy said "Hello" to the Parrot, the Parrot said "Hello" right back. Like this—

(Benjy says "Hello.")
(The Parrot says "Hello.")

"That's wonderful," said Benjy. He bought the parrot and took him home. Now he said to the bird, "What's your name?" "What's your name?" answered the Parrot. Like this:

(Benjy says, "What's your name?")
(The Parrot says, "What's your name?")

"No, no," said Benjy. "I'm asking you. What's your name?" But again the Parrot could only repeat, "What's your name?" "Oh, dear," said Benjy. "I see that my parrot can only repeat what I said." Then Benjy had a good idea.

"I'll bet we can sing 'A Needle and Thread' together." Of course, the Parrot couldn't answer with the right words, so they sang the song with "la."

Play the piano or other pitched instrument as some of the neighbors sing with Benjy and some sing with the Parrot:

Benjy and the Parrot liked that so much that they asked the Neighbors in to sing with them, and everybody sang it every day. Some sang with Benjy and some sang with the Parrot.

(Benjy and the Parrot sing with "la." The neighbors sing, too.—)

The End

Lesson 25

Merry October

Allegro

Red leaves, yel - low leaves, bright and gay,

That is what I see, Fall - ing from the tree.

Lesson 25
MERRY OCTOBER

1   Yesterday as I walked home, I could tell that the summer was over. Can you tell me what I saw?

> Possible responses: the summer flowers are gone, the sky is different, the leaves are changing color and falling from the trees.
>
> Have the children move like leaves blown by the wind.
>
> Play the drum as the wind blows. Start slowly and then play faster and faster as the leaves whirl around and finally fall down. (This can be done several times.)

2

> Put two leaves on the board, one red and the other yellow. (Space them far apart.)

Here, by the yellow leaf, is a pump that gives us yellow paint. Let's kneel down and pump some out.

> Have the children kneel and say "yel-low yel-low" as they make the pumping gesture.
>
> *Yel-low* (Pump Pump)
> *Yel-low* (Pump Pump)
>
> Play the same with the drum.

3   How many sounds go together in "yel-low?" Right. It's fun to find other words that have two sounds, too. Everybody think of one to go with "yel-low."

> *Yel-low* (Pump Pump)
> *Bel-low* (Pump Pump)
>
> Give as many individual children as possible a turn.

4   Now let's pump some red paint.

> Have the children kneel on the floor by the red leaf on the board (some distance from the yellow leaf).
>
> All say "red" as they again make the strong pumping gesture.
>
> *Red* (Pump)
> *Red* (Pump)
>
> Play the drum part of the time.

5   We can hear that "red" has one sound. "Bed" goes with "red." What else?

> *Red* (Pump)
> *Bed* (Pump)
>
> Give as many individual children as possible a turn to say their own new word. Any word or any nonsense word of one syllable is good.

6   Sometimes we have to go from the yellow pump to the red pump and back again.

> Play the drum for *yel-low:* ♫
>
> or *red:* ♩
>
> Have the children pump at yellow or red as you change the drum rhythm. Vary the time spent at each pump.
>
> Put the running notes on the board: ♫

7

Good. Here on the board is the music sign for the rhythm of "yel-low." I'll draw another walking note and then we can say "yel-low leaves."

Draw on the board:

Give individual children a turn to go to the board and point to the notes as they say "yel-low leaves."

8

Place a varied group of note cards face up on a flat surface, with enough running note cards and walking note cards for each child.

Have each child pick out a running note card.

Will you run now while I play the running notes on the drum? When I play anything else, stop and wait until the running notes come again.

Play ♩♩, etc., on the drum, alternating with ♩, etc. The children wait when you play the ♩ notes, then run again when you play ♩♩.

9

The children are seated.

Draw a walking note on the board.

This is the music sign for "red," our walking note. I'll draw another walking note on the board and then we can say "red leaves."

Draw on the board:

♩ ♩

Give individual children a turn to go to the board and point to the notes as they say "red leaves."

10

Place varied note cards face up on a flat surface, with enough walking note cards for each child.

Red leaves make a wonderful walking song. First, exchange your running note card for a walking note card.

Good. Let's see how many walking note songs we can make up. Listen—

Sing one phrase, very simple and short, such as "Red leaves, red leaves, on a tree." Then all walk as they sing the same, "Red leaves, red leaves, on a tree." Walk and sing with the children.

Now have one child walk and sing his or her own song, perhaps "I see red leaves on a tree," as everyone else waits and listens.

Then everyone walks and sings the same, "I see red leaves on a tree."

Note: Encourage any effort, however slight. Two or three songs are sufficient at one lesson.

11

The children are seated.

This is a song about red *and* yellow leaves.

Sing the song and teach it to the children.

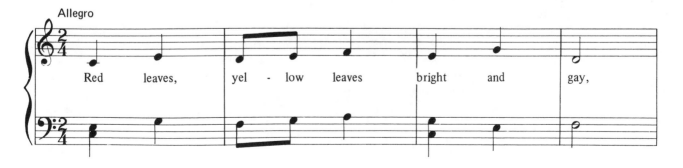

12 **This is a good walking song, too. Let's all walk as we sing the new song.**

> Play as all the children walk and sing.

13 **When all the leaves have fallen from the tree, we know the winter is here. Soon, icicles will hang from the branches and snow will be on the ground.**
Show me how you think the tree will look in the winter.

> Have the children stand like a tree in the winter. Make the sound of the cold wind with your voice: "oooooooh, oooooooh," and encourage the children to look and feel "cold."

14 **But spring comes after winter. All the trees are covered with green leaves. I'll play while your branches swing.**

> Play on the piano or another pitched instrument:

15 **Good. While I read you this story about the month of October, think about which part you would like to act out.**

Story Time

Read the story aloud to the children. Then read it aloud again as the individual parts are carried out in movement and song by the children.

Characters
The month of October
The month of January
The month of May
The Sun
The People who live
near the trees

Once upon a time, the month of October was in great trouble. He had many cans of brown and red paint, but his cans of yellow paint were empty. And only part of the leaves had been painted.

"I will ask my friends for help," he thought, and he flew to the month of January.

(October flies to January.)

January was standing like an icicle, frozen and stiff.

Play the drum:

♩♪ ♩♪ ♩♪ ♩♪ *etc.*

(January stands like an icicle.)

"I would like to help you," said January, "but you see I have only white paint."

Then October flew to see the month of May.

(October flies to May.)

Play the drum:

May waved her arms softly like a spring breeze.

(May waves her arms softly.)

Play the drum softly:

"I would gladly give you a share of what I have," said May gently, "but I have only green paint. Why don't you ask the Sun?"

So October flew to see the Sun.

(October flies to the Sun.)

Play the drum:

The Sun was riding in the sky with his arms overhead.

(The Sun moves slowly with arms overhead.)

Play the drum slowly:

"Why not?" he said. "Take as much as you need."

October was happy. He took two great pails of yellow and went home.

Then he painted the leaves.

(October paints the leaves.)

Play the drum:

Play as the people walk and sing:

Everyone said it was the most beautiful fall they had ever seen. Then they sang the special October song as they walked among the trees.

The End

Lesson 26

Happy New Year

© 1982 by The Center for Applied Research in Education, Inc.

Brightly

Mer - ry are the bells, I hear them

call, Hap - py New Year to one and all!

Ding, dong, Ding, dong, Ding, ding, Dong.____

136

Lesson 26
HAPPY NEW YEAR

1 I think we have just enough time to get ready for the New Year. First we have to run to the store to buy a new broom so we can make everything fresh and shining. When the music stops, buy your broom and then we'll bring it home.

Have the children run to the store to buy a new broom. Interrupt the music to give the children time to "buy" the broom.

Play Record 41-6097 S7B1 (Piano No. 15).

2 Now for a good sweeping. We mustn't forget to clean the windows and rub the pots and pans.

Have the children move freely as they perform any tasks in preparation for the holiday.

Play Record 41-6091 S4B1 (Piano No. 8).

3 We need a song to welcome the New Year. Everyone likes this one. Listen—

Sing the song and teach it to the children.

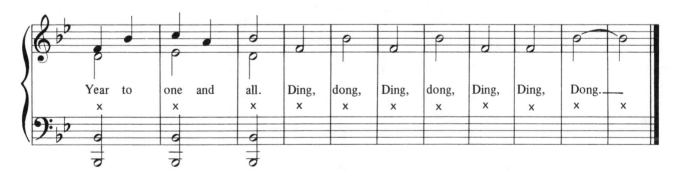

4

Obtain a picture of a large church bell to show the children.

First, let's see how the big bell moves.

Describe the big bell—very heavy, it rings when the rope is pulled.

It's such a big bell that it rings very slowly. Let's swing as we sing our song.

Swing forward and back with the children (or side to side) as you all sing the song (seated). The swing is slow, marked *x* in the song:

Swing	*Swing*
Merry are the	bells, I
hear them	call,

5   Now we can pull the rope while we sing again.

Have all the children "pull the bell rope" in the same rhythm as for activity 4 above, while singing.

Merry are the bells, I
(Pull down)   (Up)

Encourage a long pull going down, as the knees bend.
Play the piano or another pitched instrument.

6

You will need a large cymbal with a drumstick.

(Amy), will you play the big bell on the cymbal, when it sings "Ding, dong, ding, dong, ding, ding, dong?"

Have all the children sing the song. At "Ding, dong, ding, dong, ding, ding, dong," they pull the bell rope as in activity 5 while one child plays the cymbal, marked *x* in the song. (The cymbal is struck with a drumstick.)

7   Good. Some people live very far away from the town. When they hear the song and the bells, it sounds very, very soft and very far away. Let's all sing and play again, and see how far away we can make it sound.

Have all the children sing and "pull the rope" as for activity 6, but now as softly as possible. One child joins with the cymbal, played lightly, at "Ding, dong, ding, dong, ding, ding, dong."
Play the piano or other pitched instrument very softly and with a far-off sound.

8

Give all the children finger cymbals.

On New Year's Day everyone comes out to say "Happy New Year" to their friends. Sometimes they sing the New Year's song and play their finger cymbals as they walk.

Will you walk now? Play your cymbals as you sing, too. If you hear the music stop, it means you've met some friends. Stop singing and say "Happy New Year" to them. When you hear the music again, walk and sing again. Play your cymbals, too.

To produce a more resonant sound, strike the edge of one cymbal with the flat surface of the other.
Have the children pay the cymbals freely as they step.
Play the first phrase of the song on the piano or another pitched instrument. Stop and wait for the children to greet each other. Then play to the end of the song as the children walk, sing, and play the finger cymbals. Stop and wait again for the children to greet each other.
Now you might play from the beginning to the end of the song while the children again walk, sing, and play the finger cymbals.

9

Put a slow note, 𝅗𝅥 , and a walking note 𝅘𝅥 , on the chalkboard, drawn very large and spaced far apart.

These are the music signs for the big slow bell and the walking bell. Listen as I play and move like the bell I'm playing. Pull the rope for the big slow bell, or walk with the walking bell notes. When I stop playing, go to the board and point to the music sign for the bell you just did.

or

10 At the New Year's party, everyone skips. You can, too. Take a partner if you wish.

Play Record 41-6093 S8B2 (Piano No. 6).

Story Time

Characters
Chief Bell Ringer
Shopkeeper
A Tiny Bell
A Medium-Sized Bell
The Biggest Bell
All the People

Read the story aloud to the children. Then read it aloud again as the individual parts are carried out in movement and song by the children.

Play the drum for fast walking:

♩ ♩ ♩ ♩ ♩ *etc.*

(Finger cymbals)

(Can be played on a xylophone)

Play the drum:

♫ ♫ ♫ ♫ *etc.*

It was getting later and later. The New Year was waiting just outside the door. Soon it would be time for the Chief Bell Ringer to ring in the New Year.

But the Big Bell was nowhere to be found! "How can I let in the New Year if I have no bell to ring?" cried the Chief Bell Ringer.

He hurried to the Bell Store.

(The Chief Bell Ringer hurries to the store.)

"Please," he said. "I would like a bell for ringing in the New Year."

"How about this one?" asked the Shopkeeper. He held out a tiny bell that went "ding, dong, ding, dong."

(The Shopkeeper plays the Tiny Bell.)

"Oh, no," said the Chief Bell Ringer. "The New Year would never hear that."

"Here's another," the Shopkeeper said. And he showed one that went, "Ding, Dong, Ding, Dong."

(The shopkeeper plays the Medium-Sized Bell.)

"No, no. Something *bigger*," cried out the Chief Bell Ringer.

"This is the biggest one I have," said the Shopkeeper. The Big Bell rang out.

(The shopkeeper plays a large cymbal with a drumstick.)

"*That's it!*" the Chief Bell Ringer exclaimed. He ran back with the Big Bell.

(The Bell Ringer runs back with the Big Bell.)

He was just in time to let the New Year in, as everyone sang and the bell tolled.

140

Play as all the people
sing and the Bell tolls.
The Bell Ringer plays
the cymbal at Ding,
Dong, (marked *x*)

The End

Hurry Up!

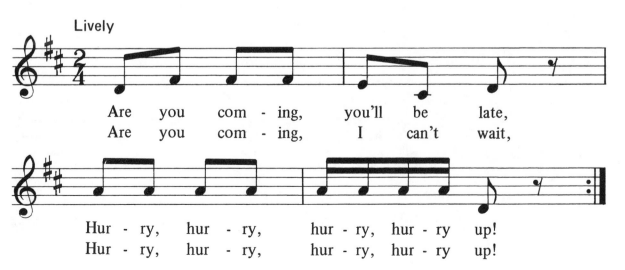

Lively

Are you com - ing, you'll be late,
Are you com - ing, I can't wait,

Hur - ry, hur - ry, hur - ry, hur - ry up!
Hur - ry, hur - ry, hur - ry, hur - ry up!

Lesson 27
HURRY UP!

1   One day I was walking home with some ice cream in a bag. Will you walk with me?
>All the children walk freely with you.

Then I saw that the ice cream was beginning to melt. What do you think I did? Right! I hurried up. Will you show me how you "hurry up?"
>Have the children walk to show how they "hurry up" (free movement).

2
>The children are seated.

When I came home, Mother was baking a cake. The dough had to be mixed. Let's mix it together.
>"Mix the dough" with the children, using a circular movement in a rather slow tempo.

Mother called out, "The oven's ready. Please hurry up." Show me how you hurry up.
>Have the children "hurry up" to get the dough mixed.

3   Good. We all hurry up when we're late for school. Listen to the drum as you get ready to go. First, you think you have lots of time. Then you see the clock. You'd better "hurry up."
>Have the children show any "before school" preparation in free movement—getting dressed, eating breakfast, putting books together.
>Play the drum in a walking tempo. Then play faster until you are playing in a "hurried" tempo.

4
>Give the children rhythm sticks. All are seated.

Here's a fun way to tell a story we know. First, we'll play our sticks as we say:
>(Show), playing rhythm sticks on x
>Eeny Meeny Miney Mo
>x   x   x   x
>
>Catch a tiger by the toe,
>x   x   x   x
>
>If he hollers let him go,
>x   x   x   x
>
>Eeny Meeny Miney Mo.
>x   x   x   x
>
>Have all the children do the same as you repeat.

Now we'll start the same way, but when we get to "If he hollers," we'll hurry to the end.
>Now do the rhyme with the children, playing the rhythm sticks. Start in a moderate tempo but get faster until you are in a "hurried" tempo.
>Try it once or twice starting in the same moderate tempo but getting very fast and finishing as fast as possible.

5   That was very good. Now let's hurry up in the middle of a song we know.
>Sing a well-known song with the children, such as "I'm Going Up," "High-Stepping Horses," or "The Farmer in the Dell," starting in a moderate tempo and getting faster to hurry to the end.

6   That was fun, too. Here's a song about "Hurry Up." You might want to sing it to a friend.

Sing the song and teach it to the children.

7   (Benjy), you can conduct, standing in front. Everyone else will do the same, conducting beats in their seats while we sing "Hurry, hurry."

Give one child a turn to conduct standing in front of the children and holding a conductor's stick or baton, as everyone sings again. Then have all the children do the same, conducting beats in their seats as they sing.

In this song, the conductor's beat goes down-up (marked in song).

8   Now let's sing our song while we make the running note sounds on our knees.

With the children, tap with an open hand, palm down on each knee, singing:

Left	*Right*
Are	you
com-	ing,
you'll	be
late,	𝄾
Hur-	ry,
Hur-	ry,
Hurry,	hurry
up!	𝄾

9   Good. I'll play while you run. Sing the song to yourself while you are running and see if you can stop right on the word "up!"

We'll try it out first while you're standing. I'll play the song while you sing it to yourself. Have your hands ready to clap in front of you, and come in with a loud clap on "up!"

Play the song as the children sing it to themselves, and give a strong clap on "up!"

Repeat if necessary.

Then, as you play the song, have all the children run, singing the song to themselves and stopping as well as possible on "up!"

144

Story Time

Characters
The Little Rain Cloud
Mrs. Jones
The Farmer
The Sun
Children at school

Play the drum:

♫ ♫ ♫ ♫ *etc.*

Play the drum slowly:

♩ ♩ ♩ ♩ *etc.*

Play the drum for a fast walk (hurried):

♩ ♩ ♩ ♩ *etc.*

Play the drum:

♫ ♫ ♫ ♫ *etc.*

Play the drum slowly:

♩ ♩ ♩ *etc.*

Play the drum for a fast walk (hurried):

♩ ♩ ♩ ♩ *etc.*

Play the drum for a quickened run (hurried):

♫ ♫ ♫ *etc.*

All the children at school sing.

Read the story aloud to the children. Then read it aloud again as the individual parts are carried out in movement and song by the children.

Once upon a time, there was a Little Rain Cloud who was very mischievous. What he liked best was to find people who didn't expect him and to see them hurry to get out of his way.

One fine Sunday afternoon, he went sailing through the sky.

(The Little Rain Cloud sails through the sky.)

He stopped when he saw Mrs. Jones out walking in her best Sunday hat. Mrs. Jones was walking slowly as she looked in all the shop windows.

(Mrs. Jones looks in the shop windows.)

"Oh dear," she said as she saw the Little Rain Cloud. "I mustn't let my Sunday hat get wet. I'd best hurry home!" And she did.

(Mrs. Jones hurries home.)

"Ha, ha!" laughed the Little Rain Cloud. He floated further in the sky.

(The Little Rain Cloud floats farther.)

He stopped again when he saw a Farmer carrying a heavy bale of hay. The load was heavy and the Farmer walked slowly.

(The Farmer walks slowly, carrying the heavy bale.)

"Oh, oh," said the Farmer as he saw the Little Rain Cloud. "If it rains my hay will be spoiled. I'll have to hurry to the barn." And he did.

(The Farmer hurries to the barn.)

"Ha, ha!" laughed the Little Rain Cloud again. But wait! As he looked up he saw that the Sun was coming out!

"Oh, oh!" he said. "Time for *me* to hurry away." And he did.

(The Little Rain Cloud hurriedly runs away.)

The next day at school, all the children sang this song:

The End

Lesson 28

Little Feather

Please bring rain, please bring rain, Oh Great One, please bring rain.

Lesson 28
LITTLE FEATHER

1   Little Feather was the name of a very young Indian boy. Sometimes his father would take him hunting with a bow and arrow.

He had to learn to step very slowly and softly, then all at once to run very fast and very lightly. Sometimes he must just stand still, as still as a tree.

I'll play on the drum while we do some of these things together. The music will tell you how to move.

Have the children move as you play the drum. Vary the length of each rhythm by repeating more or less. Alternate between the different rhythms.

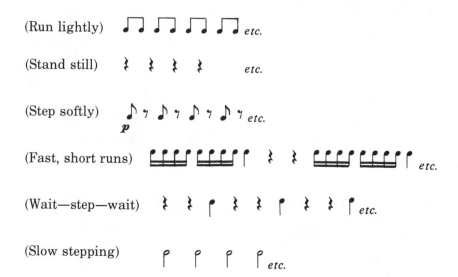

2   **Indians like to imitate the animals, too. Here, Little Feather is watching a deer.**

Have individual children act out the movements of a deer (freely). Encourage any original efforts.

Probable responses: runs, looks around, nibbles leaves, drinks from a brook, stands and listens.

3   **Good. All the Indian children were given names that were the same as things that they loved. It could be the name of a deer, like Running Deer, or the name of a bird, like Flying Eagle. Sometimes it was the name of a river, like Flowing River, or the name of the sky, like Blue Sky.**

Think of a name you would like for yourself. When I point to you, stand up and say who you are. Like this: "I am Flying Eagle." Then, if you want to, you can show us how Flying Eagle walks around the village.

Give as many children as possible a turn to tell their Indian name and, if they wish, to walk around the village as an Indian might.

You can play the drum as accompaniment for the walking.

4   **Sometimes the Indian's corn needed more rain. Then everyone prayed to the Great Spirit. They had a special song and dance for this. Listen to the song and the drum beat that goes with it.**

Sing the song as you beat the drum (marked *x* in the song). Then teach it to the children.

Pesante

Please bring rain, please bring rain, Oh Great One, please bring rain.

5 Good. Everyone kneel down now and make the drum beat on the floor with your hands. We'll sing the song, too. If I call your name, come up and play the drum until I call someone else's name.

Have all the children kneel and sing as they make the drum beat on the floor with their hands. Call individual children up to play the drum.
The song can be repeated two or three times.

6 Copy the song in large notes on the chalkboard.

These are the music signs for our Indian song. The drum beat that goes with it is like a walking note.

Draw the walking note with the stem down (down because there is another note on top). Put a walking note—the drum beat—under the first two notes of the song.
Then all the children sing "Please bring rain," as they clap to find the two drum beats in "rain." Have individual children add a walking note on the board.

On board:

Children add: ♩ ♩ ♩ ♩ *etc.*

7 Good. I think we can do the dance now.

Have the children step firmly, leaning slightly forward, as they go in a circle. The dance has the same steps throughout the song.

L	R	L	
Step	Step	Hold	____
R	L	R	
Step	Step	Hold	____

Play the drum as marked *x* in the song. Say, "Step Step Hold ____," as the children step.

8 (Benjy), you can play the drum now, while we all sing and dance. Remember that you really need the rain or there will be nothing to eat.

Play the song on the piano or another pitched instrument as the children sing and dance and one child plays the drum.
The song and dance can be repeated (the children reverse direction) with a different child playing the drum.

9 The children are seated.

This is an easy song to play on the piano (or xylophone). First let's tap it on our knees.

Have the children tap on their knees with an open palm, face down, as they say the words of the song:

Please bring rain,
R   L   L
Please bring rain,
R   L   L
Oh   Great One,
R   L   L
Please bring rain.
R   L   L

10 (Amy), come play it on the piano.

Show all the children how (Amy) will start on E♭, and skip one note as she plays and sings.

E♭	C	C	____
Right	Left	Left	
Please	bring	rain	____
E♭	C	C#	
Right	Left	Left	
Please	bring	rain	____
E♭	C	C#	
Right	Left	Left	
Oh	Great	One,	____
E♭	C	C#	
Right	Left	Left	
Please	bring	rain.	____

Give other children a turn to play and sing. (Use two sticks, one in each hand, if you use a xylophone.)

11 Good. Now we'll do our Rain Song and Dance again.

A different child can play the drum. Play as for activity 4 above, on the piano or another pitched instrument.

Story Time

Characters
Little Feather
Little Feather's Friends
The Indians in the
  village

Play the piano or other
pitched instrument as
the drum plays and the
Indians dance and sing:

Read the story aloud. Then read it aloud again as the individual parts are carried out in movement and song by the children.

Once upon a time there was a little Indian boy. His name was Little Feather. He lived in the Indian village with his mother and father.

The men in the village were great hunters. They also planted many fields of corn. Sometimes it happened that it did not rain for many weeks and the land was very dry.

Then all the Indians did a song and dance to ask the Rain Spirit for rain. It went like this—

(The Indians do the rain song and dance.)

Please bring rain, please bring rain, Oh Great One, please bring rain.

Little Feather and his friends always watched very carefully. One day they said, "Let's do the Rain Song and Dance by ourselves." One Indian boy played the drum while everyone else sang and danced.

Play again as above as
Little Feather and his
Friends play the drum
and sing and dance.

(Little Feather and his Friends do the rain song and dance.)

That night the rain came. It rained and rained and rained, and it kept on raining.

"Oh, oh," said all the people. "The crops of corn will be ruined. Who has brought this rain?"

Now Little Feather and his friends were very sorry. They told their parents what they had done. So all the people did a special song and dance to ask, "Please let the sun come out."

When they saw the sun, Little Feather and his friends knew they were forgiven. They said, "We'll never do *that* again! And they never did.

The End

Lesson 29

Spring

Allegretto

I hear him sing, Tu - weet tu-

weet, he comes to tell us it ___ is Spring.

Lesson 29
SPRING

1   This seems like a special morning to run together with the music. Go lightly. If the music stops "high," put your arms up high as you stop. If the music stops "low," bend over just a little as you stop.

> Have the children run as you play. Alternate between stopping high and low, as high, low—high, high—low, high—low, low. Encourage the children to run lightly on their toes.

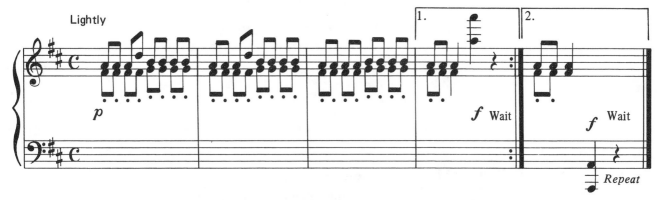

2   I know why it's a special morning. On the way to school I saw a bluebird. I could tell that winter was going away and the warm spring would soon be here. What will the spring bring?

> Probable responses: warm sun, flowers, many leaves on the trees, spring rain, soft grass, birds.
> Have the children move freely as any of the things named, all at the same time.
> Play Record 41-6094 S1B4 (Piano No. 28).

3   The Spring Fairy is like a magician. Lots of things change when she comes. In the nest in the tree there's a robin's egg. What happens in the spring?

> Talk about how the bird comes out of the egg.
> Have the children roll themselves up like an egg on the floor. When they hear the flying music, it's time for them to come out of their shells and "fly."
> Play Record 41-6087 S3B1 (Piano No. 23) for "flying."

4   Good. Now here's a tree in winter, all frozen and bare. The cold wind is howling around. What happens when the Spring Fairy comes?

> Have the children begin like the trees in winter, holding themselves stiff and with arms outstretched at angles for branches. (You can go around and feel to see how "frozen" the branches are.)
> Play on the piano or another pitched instrument:

Now the spring comes, with its gentle rain and warm sun. Green leaves grow from all the branches. While the music plays, move your branches softly.

Play Record 41-6094 S1B4 (Piano No. 28).

5   All the seeds are waiting in the ground to come up. Everyone can be a seed in the ground. When you hear the music going up, that's the time for you to come up, too.

Have the children roll themselves up into "seeds" on the floor. They stay still until they hear you play on the piano or another pitched instrument:

6   Good. We mustn't forget the big brown Bear. All winter he's been sleeping in his cave, waiting for spring. Now he knows it's time to come out.

Ask the children to suggest different ways that the Bear might know it's spring.

Probable responses: he gets warm, he gets hungry, the Spring Fairy sends a messenger.

Play the record for the Bear, as the children move: 41-6088 S5B4 (Piano No. 5).

7   Listen. Maybe the bluebird was the Spring Fairy's messenger.

Sing the song and teach it to the children.

8   All the children have handballs.

Our spring song is especially good to sing when we're on the playground.

Have the children pass the ball from one hand to the other as they sing. Encourage them to put the ball into the opposite hand on the beat of the song (marked *x* in the song).

Play the song as in activity 7 above.

9   You will need one very large ball.
Have all the children make a circle.
Use two large balls and two circles if more suitable for spacing.

This time, pass the ball to the person on your right. If I play the song slowly, you have more time. Take the ball a little up in the air if you have to. Like this—

(Show.) (Ball is held with two hands.) When you play slowly, the ball can go—

I hear   him sing,   tu-weet,

When you play fast, the ball must go directly in a shorter line—

I hear him sing, Tu-weet,

Play the song on the piano or any pitched instrument as in activity 7. Play it very slowly, then several times again, either slowly or fast.

10   Give each child a skipping note card ♩ ♪

On your card is the music sign for skipping. Everybody can skip now as you sing the spring song.

> Play the song twice. The first time, have the children hold the card up in one hand. The second time, have the children reverse direction and hold the card up in the other hand.
>
> Play as for activity 7.

Story Time

Characters
Benjy
Benjy's Friends
The Spring Fairy
The Egg, which turns
  into the Bird
The Sun
The Apple Tree
The Gentle Wind
The Spring Rains
(Sign: "Spring Magic
Show")

> Read the story aloud. Then read it aloud again as the individual parts are carried out in movement and song by the children.

Once upon a time, Benjy walked down his street and sniffed the air. Gosh, it was good. He could tell spring was coming.

There was a sign at the end of the block. "Spring Magic Show," it said. Benjy saw some of his friends go in. He went in, too.

The Spring Fairy was the teacher. "Here we have an Egg," she said.

The Egg was all curled around on the ground as eggs are when they are in the nest.

(The Egg is curled up on the floor.)

The Spring Fairy waved her wand as she continued speaking. "Now the Sun comes to make it warm."

In came the Sun to stand near the Egg.

Play the drum:

♩   ♩ *etc.*

(The Sun enters and stands near the Egg.)

Now, as everyone watched, the Egg opened and out came a baby Bird. "Tweet, tweet," it sang as it flew around.

Play the drum or triangle:

♫ ♫ *etc.*

(The Egg, now a bird, comes up and flies around, singing "Tu-weet, Tu-weet.")

"That was certainly magical," said Benjy. He went home. In his front yard was an apple tree. Little green buds were to be seen on all the branches.

(The Apple Tree stands.)

Soon the Gentle Wind blew.

(The wind enters and swings her arms slowly and gently.)

Play the drum:

♫♫ ♫♫ *etc.*
3   3

The Spring Rains brought water.

(The Spring Rains bring water.)

Play the drum:

♬♬ ♬♬ ♫ *etc.*

The Sun brought warmth.

(The Sun enters, arms overhead.)

Play the drum:

♩ ♩ ♩ ♩ *etc.*

Now Benjy made a sign, "Spring Magic Show," just like the one the Spring Fairy had. He hung the sign on the apple tree.

(Benjy hangs the sign on the tree.)

Soon the buds blossomed into great pink and white flowers. All of Benjy's friends came to see the tree. They could hardly believe what they saw. Benjy could hardly believe it himself.

"That was certainly magical," he said. And then Benjy and his friends sang the special spring song.

Play as Benjy and his friends sing:

I hear him sing, Tu-weet, tu-weet, he comes to tell us it __ is Spring.

The End

The Muffin Man

Moderato

English Folk Song

Oh, do you know the Muf-fin Man, the Muf-fin Man, the
Oh, yes, I know the Muf-fin Man, the Muf-fin Man, the

Muf - fin Man, Oh, do you know the
Muf - fin Man, Oh, yes, I know the

Muf - fin Man, who lives in Dru - ry Lane?
Muf - fin Man, who lives in Dru - ry Lane.

Lesson 30
THE MUFFIN MAN

1   **This morning I had some delicious muffins for breakfast. I bought them from the Muffin Man. Every day he pushes a cart filled with muffins. He sings as he walks along, so that the people will know he is coming.**

   I'll play the Muffin Man's song. You can walk along the way he does, pushing his cart.

Play on the piano or another pitched instrument as the children walk like the Muffin Man:

2   The children are seated.

   Good. Listen to the Muffin Man's song. See if you can tell me what the question is, and then what the answer is.

Sing and play both verses of the song, as in activity 1 above, for question-and-answer recognition.

   In this song, is the melody the same for the question and the answer or is it different?

Sing and play the two verses of the song for recognition of the same melody for both verses.

3   Teach the song to the children.

4   Divide the seating into two sections.

   Now everyone can choose. Sit with the question singers or the answer singers.

Have the children sit in either the question or answer section.

Play the song as in activity 1 as each group sings either the question or the answer. Then have the children change seats and parts and repeat the song.

5   If we wanted to help the Muffin Man sell his muffins, we might go along with him and call out "Buy some _now_."

> The children now step and call out:
>
> "Buy some _now_" (accent on _now_)
>
> ♩ ♩ ♩
>
> "Buy some _now_"
>
> ♩ ♩ ♩
>
> Play the drum in the same rhythm and call out with the children as they step. Repeat as many times as desirable.

6   Let's do that again. But now, if I call your name, come and play the drum while you say "Buy some _now_" with everyone else. When I call another name, go back and step again.

> Have the children repeat activity 5. Give individual children a turn to play the drum (♩ ♩ ♩) while the others continue to step and call out "Buy some _now_."
>
> Play with the rhythm sticks in the same rhythm and call out with the children as they step.

7

> The children are seated.

(Amy), play the drum and say "Buy some _now_" while we sing the Muffin Man's song.

> Play the song as for activity 1. Have the children sing while one child plays the drum and says "Buy some _now_" at the same time.
>
> Give several children a turn with the drum.

8   Good. I think we should make some melodies of our own to ask, "Do you know the Muffin Man?" Listen first. Which way is my voice going, up or down?

> Speak in a well-defined rise:
>
>
>
> "Do you know the Muffin Man?"
>
> Have a child repeat the question and put a line going upward on the chalkboard.

9

> Give several children turns to play the question, "Do you know the Muffin Man?" on any black notes of the piano or xylophone, going upward. Have them sing the words while playing.
>
> Encourage playing in the middle range (because of its similarity to the voice range).

10   Sometimes the Muffin Man's friend says to him: "Coming out?"

> Repeat the "Coming out?" several times for recognition of the upward motion of the question.
>
> Give several children a turn to play the question on any black notes of the piano or xylophone. Two notes in an upward direction are sufficient as they say:
>
>
>
> "Coming out?"

158

11 Maybe he answered: "O-\
                      K"

Repeat the "O-\ several times for recognition of the downward motion
K"
of the answer.

Give several children a turn to play the answer on any black notes of the
piano or xylophone. Two notes in a downward direction are sufficient as
they say:

"O-\
    K"

12 Every night the Muffin Man has to mix the batter for the muffins and put it in the
oven. Then he has to polish his cart and count his money, to be ready for the next day.
You can do all that now.

Have the children make the muffins, polish the cart, doing any
preparations in free movement.

Play Record 41-6089 S7B1 (Piano No. 10).

Story Time

Characters
The Muffin Man
The Muffin Man's
  Friend
The Townspeople

Play the piano or
another pitched
instrument as the
Muffin Man walks and
sings the question and
his Friend plays the
drum as he says:
"Buy some *now*"

Read the story aloud. Then read it aloud again as the individual parts are carried out in movement and song by the children. Any number of children can carry out an individual part.

Once upon a time there was a man who made very good muffins, which was why he was called the Muffin Man. Every day he pushed his cart through the streets of the town to sell as many muffins as he could.

But though he tried very hard, he always came home with his muffins unsold. "What shall I do?" he cried bitterly to his friend.

"If more people heard you coming with your cart, maybe you would sell more muffins," said his friend. "Let's try this. While you push the cart and sing your song, I'll go along and play my drum to say 'Buy some *now*.'"

And that's what they did. It sounded like this—

(The Muffin Man pushes his cart and sings the first verse as his Friend plays on the drum.)

Play the piano or
another pitched
instrument as the
people walk about and
sing the answer to the
song.

Now all the people opened their windows to hear the music, and when they saw the delicious muffins they ran out to buy them.

(All the people run out to buy muffins.)

Soon everyone was singing the answer to the Muffin Man's song and eating muffins as they walked about the town.

(The children sing the second verse, without the drum, as they walk about.)

I am glad to say that the Muffin Man and his friend lived happily ever after.

The End

Lesson 31

Sailing

Andante

We're sail-ing on the o-cean blue, Pull, pull, pull a-gain for

that is what we like to do. Pull, pull, pull a-gain.

Lesson 31
SAILING

1 Did you hear the wind blowing last night? It must be fun to be the wind going everywhere and making things happen.

You can move like the wind while the music plays. Then, you can tell us where you went and what happened.

Play Record 41-6093 S8B3 (Piano No. 22).

Probable responses: went down the city streets, blew hats off, made the people hurry, blew the leaves around, pushed sailboats, made the waves rise high.

2 If we had a sailboat, we would have to see that everything was just right before we took it over the ocean. What has to be done?

Probable responses: scrub the decks, paint the sides, mend the ropes, test the wheel, see that the water containers are full, see that the food is packed away.

Have the children do any task in free movement. Later, individual children can show what they did.

Play Record 41-6091 S4B3 (Piano No. 18).

3 Good. Now we're almost ready to go. But we need a captain.

Have the children walk around as the captain might, to see that all is ready.

Play a strong walking beat with the drum.

4 We need a helmsman, too, to steer the boat.

The children can act as "helmsmen," steering a big wheel. The helmsman stands with legs somewhat apart to balance himself on a moving boat.

One child can be the "lookout," calling "Straight ahead" or "Turn."

5 If it's a big boat, we'll have many sailors. First, they pull the ropes to make the sails go up.

Have each child face a partner. Both take hold of a "rope" and pull down as their knees bend.

Everyone says together, as they go down and up:

DOWN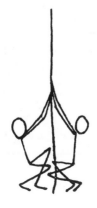

UP

6 Now we pull up the anchor.

Have the children stand in several lines, facing front. They pull the anchor rope together, going from left to right.

Everyone says together as they pull the rope:

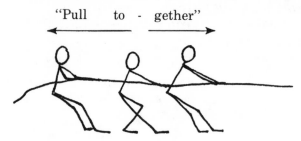

7 If we sing while we pull the ropes, we would be *sure* to pull together. This is a song that all sailors like to sing. Listen—

Sing the song and teach it to the children.

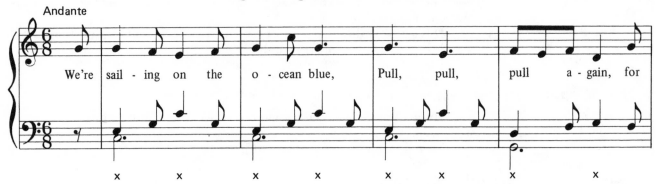

8 Now we can pull the sails up while we sing.

Have each child take a partner. All pull the ropes together as they go up and down. Going down their knees bend, going up their knees straighten. The feeling is one of effort and release.

Now everyone sings as they move on the beat, marked *x* on the song:

9 We'll sing while we pull the anchor up, too.

> All the children pull the anchor up, as in activity 6 above. They sing as they pull from left to right.

10

> Give all the children scarfs to hold as "sails." Separate ends can be held in each hand, held up at a comfortable level.

Before our boat goes sailing, the helmsman has to be at the wheel and the captain has to walk around to see that all is ready.

> Have one child be the helmsman (to steer with the big wheel, standing at one side), and one child for the captain (to walk around with a strong step to see that all is ready, then standing at one side).

Good. Now hold your sails up as the boat goes over the ocean.

> Play record 41-6088 S5B3. (Piano No. 1).
> Have the children move in the same direction, then reverse direction if desirable.

11

> All the children are seated.

Here's a sound the sailors always hear. What is it?

> Sing like the sea gull (and play on a pitched instrument):
>
> Caw Caw
> G   E

Right. A Sea gull. (Amy), will you sing a "Caw, caw" like this one?

> Sing (and play on a pitched instrument) any of these two-note combinations:
>
> | Caw | Caw | | Caw | Caw | | Caw | Caw |
> |-----|-----|---|-----|-----|---|-----|-----|
> | G | E | | G | G | | E | G |
>
> | Caw | Caw | | Caw | Caw | | Caw | Caw |
> |-----|-----|---|-----|-----|---|-----|-----|
> | E | E | | E | C | | C | C |
>
> Give individual children a turn to sing a "Caw, caw" back to you. (You can also play for this.)

12 Sometimes there's a storm at sea and we hear the thunder make great crashing sounds.
At the beginning of the storm we hear just a rumble, but soon the thunder booms out. When the sound gets softer, we know the storm is going away.

> Have individual children use two sticks, one in each hand, to tell the story of the thunder on the drum. They start as softly as possible, then get louder till the sound is as loud as possible, then gradually get softer till they stop.
> A good approximation of getting louder and softer is sufficient.

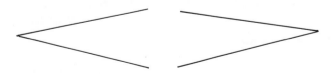

Story Time

Read the story aloud to the children. Then read it aloud again as the individual parts are carried out in movement and song by the children. One or any number of children can take an individual part.

Characters
Benjy
Sailors
One child to play the drum for thunder

Play as Benjy and all the Sailors stand facing a partner. They pull Down-Up in time with the music as they sing:

Benjy could hardly wait to get to the brook with his new sailboat. Now he sat at the water's edge and held tightly to the boat's rope. A gentle wind blew into the sails and moved the little ship back and forth.

"I wish I were a sailor," he said. He imagined himself on a great sailing ship. He was pulling the ropes with other sailors. The ropes would raise the sails. They sang, so they could pull together.

(Sailors sing and pull ropes.)

Now the boat was really moving, and Benjy could feel it riding smoothly.

(Benjy and Sailors move as if sailing.)

The wind brought storm clouds. What a noise the thunder made! How the boat rocked!

(The thunder roars and the boat rocks.)

He was glad when the storm went away and the ship once again moved smoothly.

Play the drum:

𝅘𝅥 𝅘𝅥 𝅘𝅥 𝅘𝅥 𝅘𝅥 𝅘𝅥 𝅘𝅥 𝅘𝅥 𝅘𝅥 *etc.*
p

One child plays drum very loudly to imitate thunder:

𝅘𝅥 𝅘𝅥 𝅘𝅥 𝅘𝅥 𝅘𝅥 𝅘𝅥 𝅘𝅥 𝅘𝅥 𝅘𝅥 𝅘𝅥 𝅘𝅥 𝅘𝅥 *etc.*
ff

Play the drum:

𝅘𝅥 𝅘𝅥 𝅘𝅥 𝅘𝅥 𝅘𝅥 𝅘𝅥 𝅘𝅥 𝅘𝅥 𝅘𝅥 *etc.*
p

(The boat with Benjy and the Sailors moves gently again.)

Benjy pulled on the rope, and the little ship came to shore. It was time to go home, but he would come again tomorrow. Perhaps the great sailing ship would take him far away again.

The End

Lesson 32

Over the Ice and Snow

Adapted from a
Canadian Folk Song

Allegro

Oh ____ we will go o-ver the ice and

snow, Oh ____ we will go from ____ high to low.

Lesson 32
OVER THE ICE AND SNOW

1   Early this morning as we looked out the window, we could see that the snow was falling. Could we hear it? Not a sound!
When I call your name or point to you, come out and step like a snowflake.

> Have the children initiate the movement. Call their names or point (if there are many children) until all are moving. Encourage lightness, walking on tiptoes.
> Then play Record 41-6097 S7B1 (Piano No. 15) as they continue to move freely.

2   Everyone has to help shovel snow from the path.

> Have the children make the down-up movement of shoveling snow (freely).
> Play Record 41-6088 S5B4 (Piano No. 5).

3   Now we can play. Choose a partner for a snowball fight.

> Play the drum softly as the children use the time to make a snowball. Have them throw the ball immediately after the drum plays a loud (*sfz*) beat.
>
> *Example:*

4   Good. Soon we can go skating. Let's practice.

> Have the children stand on one foot until you call "Change." Encourage them to feel how their foot presses against the floor.
> Call "Change" in the tempo of a moderate walking speed.

5   Now we'll slide one foot out at a time. Stay in time with everyone else and say "Slide, slide, slide," like this—

> Show the children a few slides:

> Have the children say "Slide" as each foot slides forward in turn—right, left, right, left.

Good. This time, put your hands behind your back and lean forward a little as you slide. Like this—

> Show the children a few slides with your hands behind your back, leaning forward a little.

6   The children are seated.

Some day, when you go ice skating in a big rink, or if you watch the skaters on TV, you will see that they skate to music. The music helps them to skate better.

Let's learn this song so we can skate better, too.

Sing the song and teach it to the children.

7 **Now, as we sing, clap and swing from side to side. That's the way your feet go when you are skating. This time, sing with "la" instead of the words.**

Sing the song again with the children, as everyone swings from side to side and claps (*x* in the song).
Sing with "la" instead of the words.

8 **Good. Listen carefully. How many times does the melody say the same thing?**

Play the phrase as it repeats three times, on the piano or another pitched instrument.
Anything to encourage the awareness of the repetitions is helpful—holding up fingers 1-2-3 as the children sing, or having the children draw three lines on the board as they sing with "la."
Then have four children stand, facing front, and each sing one phrase of the song.
Play as for activity 6 above.

9 **Now we'll skate again while we sing. Sing with "la" instead of the words.**

Play the piano or another pitched instrument and sing with the children as they skate. (Slide at *x* in the song.)
Play as for activity 6.

10 The children are seated.

I liked that. When the water in the snow gets hard, what does it turn into? Right! Icicles. Icicles are very hard. What else are they?

Probable responses: shiny, sharp, will melt if they get warm, hang from trees, come in all sizes.

Let me show you how to make icicle sounds on the piano:

Play together two notes that are next to each other—the half steps made on the piano:

Give the children turns to play several icicles on the piano, either on the same two notes or with different notes for each icicle.

Example:

Playing with one finger of each hand is usually easier for the children. Encourage them to play rather strongly and sharply.

11 If we touch the keys very lightly, we can make the snow.

Give individual children a turn to play the snowflakes on the piano or xylophone. Encourage them to touch the black keys lightly, coming down the keyboard.

12 I can tell a whole story this way—

(Show.)

(Spoken)	"Snow is falling down."
(Play)	Snowflakes as in activity 11.
(Spoken)	"Icicles are shining, too."
(Play)	Icicles as in activity 10.

I can tell a different story this way—

(Show.) Play the icicles as in activity 10 and then play the snowflakes as in activity 11.

Give individual children a turn to make their own versions of speech and music, or music alone.

13 We have a little time to go skating before we tell our story. Remember to sing the melody with "la" while you are skating.

Play the piano or another pitched instrument as in activity 6, while the children skate and sing.

Story Time

Characters
Benjy
Mr. Peters
The Skaters at the Lake

Read the story aloud. Then read it aloud again as the individual parts are carried out in movement and song by the children. One or any number of children can take an individual part.

Benjy looked in the shop window at the ice skates. The sign said "Five dollars." How he wished he could buy them! He knew there would be skating at the lake today. He walked home slowly, kicking his feet into the loose snow as he went.

Someone was calling, "Benjy." It was his neighbor, Mr. Peters.

"Benjy, would you like to shovel the snow from my walk?" he asked. "All right, answered Benjy. So all morning he went down-up, down-up with the shovel till the walk was clear and dry.

Play the drum:

(Benjy shovels the snow from the walk.)

Mr. Peters thanked Benjy and told him what a good job he had done. Then he gave him five dollars. Benjy ran straight to the store to buy the skates.

That afternoon he went skating on the lake with all his friends. Everyone was singing the skating song with "la," and his feet went "slide, slide" in time with the music. What a good time he had!

Play the piano or other pitched instrument as all the skaters sing and skate (slide with *x*):

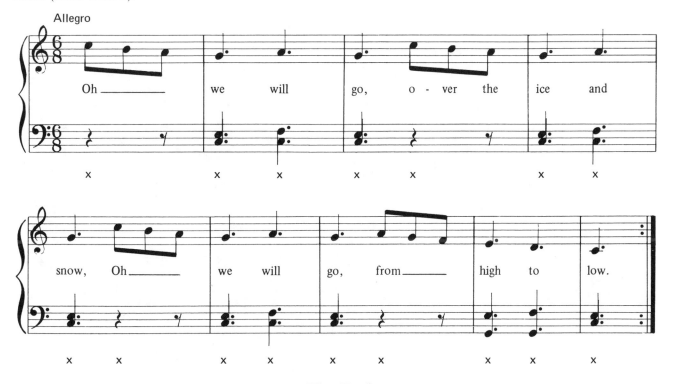

The End

Lesson 33

My Own Story

I go chug, chug, chug, I go   I say stop!

I am in the sky,   I come down.

Lesson 33
MY OWN STORY
(A Freely Improvised Lesson)

1 Let's look at your song page for today.
We see a train, a balloon, and a pony. Whichever one you choose can take you far away.

> Have one child choose a way to go—on the train, in the balloon, on the pony, or in a car. After the journey, the child shows something about the place where he or she has arrived and then comes home again.
>
> For example, (Amy) chooses to go on the train. You might play the drum for her as she moves like the train, first very slowly and then faster and faster, once around the room running smoothly and then slower till she stops.
>
> (Amy) tells everyone where she is, perhaps at the zoo, and acts out feeding the elephant. Maybe the elephant said "Thank you."
>
> She then takes the train home again, as before, from slow to fast and then slow again.
>
> Probable places the train will go: to the store, to Aunt Susie's, to the playground.
>
> Any "happening" is good, either a possible reality or fantasy.
>
> If needed, you can suggest the use of material from previous lessons. The elephant (Amy) talked to in the zoo could sing the song he knows. A pony could show how he stepped around.
>
> A very short time for each child is best, done in his or her own way without outside help.

2

> You can play the drum lightly for the child who chooses to go in the balloon.
>
> Probable places it will go: to see the giant from "Jack and the Beanstalk," to the moon, to have a race with an airplane, to give a ride to some birds.

3

> You can play the galloping rhythm on the drum for the child who chooses to go on the pony.
>
> Probable places or stories: the "cowboy" pony off to the Wild West, the racing pony going to the big race, the sheriff's pony after some bandits.
>
> If desirable in particular instances, you can encourage a feeling of a beginning, a happening, and an ending.

4 Good. We'll tell more stories next week. The train has a song that begins like this:

> "I go chug, chug, chug"
>
> Sing and play any black notes on the piano or xylophone. Then give individual children a turn to sing "I go chug, chug, chug" and to finish the song in their own way (on any black notes on the piano or xylophone).

5 The balloon has a song, too. It begins like this: "I am in the sky"

> Sing and play any black notes on the piano or xylophone. Then give individual children a turn to sing "I am in the sky," and to finish the song in their own way (on any black keys).

Story Time

Read the story aloud. Then read it aloud again as the individual parts are carried out in movement and song by the children. One or any number of children can take an individual part.

Characters
Benjy
Amy
Janie
Joshua
(Song pages of "High-Stepping Horses" and "I Go Up" mounted on large cardboard)

Benjy and his class were getting ready for Parent's Day. Everyone wanted to show something different.

"How about this?" said Benjy. "We'll put our song pages up in the room and then we'll choose the one we want to sing and act out. There'll be a table with instruments in the corner, too, in case anybody wants to play one."

"I'll try mine out," said Amy. She went over and pointed to the "High-Stepping Horses" song page.

(Amy points to the song page.)

First she showed the High-Stepping Horse out eating his breakfast.

(Amy shows the horse eating.)

Then she stepped very high as she sang "High-Stepping Horses."

(Amy steps high and sings.)

Play the piano or other pitched instrument as Amy sings:

High step-ping hors-es, All in a ring, Go step-ping, step-ping as we sing.

Now she galloped around the room two times before she sat down.

Play the drum:

♩ ♪♩ ♪ *etc.*

(Amy gallops and then sits down.)

"That's great," everyone called out.
Janie pointed to the song page for "I'm Going Up."

(Janie points to the song page.)

Then she tried out her Jack-in-the-box. She went up and down lots of different ways, sometimes slowly, sometimes very fast. Once she stayed down so long that everyone wondered, "Is she stuck in the box?" When she went up, she called out "Up." When she went down, she called out "Down."

Play the piano or another pitched instrument going up and down with Janie.

(Janie goes up and down like the Jack-in-the-box.)

Then she sang "I'm going Up." One arm went up and down as she sang.

(Janie sings.)

Play the piano or other
pitched instrument as
Janie sings:

I'm go - ing up, I'm go - ing up, And at the top I

think I'll stop, la la la la la la la la.

At the end she rolled herself up into the box again.

(Janie rolls herself into the "Box.")

One child sings his or
her own song about the
balloon as he or she
plays on the black keys
of the xylophone.

"Good, good," said Benjy and Amy. Then Joshua sang the song about a balloon that he had made up as he played on the black keys of the xylophone. It started like this: "I am in the sky."

All the parents thought the show was wonderful.

The End

At the Toy Shop

Dolce

Lav - en - der's blue, dil - ly dil - ly, Lav - en - der's green,

When I am king, dil - ly dil - ly, you shall be queen.

Lesson 34
AT THE TOY SHOP

1   This morning we're going to the toy shop. It's about four blocks away. When I play skipping notes on the drum, you walk. When I play walking notes on the drum, you skip. Like this—

> Have the children walk as you play skipping notes on the drum and say "Walk, walk, walk" to help. Then the children skip as you play walking notes on the drum and say "Skip, skip, skip" to help.
> Now play the drum without speaking, alternating the rhythms.

2   That was a good way to get to the toy shop. Maybe the shopkeeper is putting stuffed animals in the window so everyone can see what he has in the shop.

> Mark off a small section of the room to be the "window space," with perhaps a few chairs set out.
> Have individual children (the number depending on the space) move like the animal or toy they want to be and take a place in the window space. They can sit on the floor or on a chair just as they might be in a window display.
> All the other children can "look in the window" to see the display.

3   We go inside the shop. A sign says "Special Today. A Dancing Bear right from the Circus. Comes in with his own Music Box."

> All of the children can find the picture of Dancing Bear on the song sheet.

We'd better learn Dancing Bear's music.

> Sing the song and teach it to the children.

4 We can clap and swing while we sing, too, slowly and easily like Dancing Bear.

Clap and swing with the children. (The claps are marked *x* in the song.)

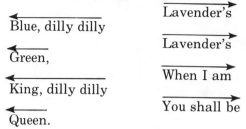

←
Blue, dilly dilly

←
Green,

←
King, dilly dilly

←
Queen.

Lavender's →

Lavender's →

When I am →

You shall be →

5

Draw 𝅗𝅥. on the chalkboard.

This is the music sign for the claps we just did. It's the slow note we know, with a dot after it.

In Dancing Bear's song, three sounds go together to make the slow note with a dot. This time when we swing and clap, let's sing "1, 2, 3." Like this—

Swing and clap as you sing (clap marked x).

Repeat as all the children swing and clap with you, singing 1, 2, 3:

Swing 1, 2, 3   1, 2, 3, etc.
←   →

Give individual children turns to draw the dotted half note (dotted slow note) on the board.

6 (Benjy), will you turn the music box handle while we all dance like Dancing Bear, slowly and easily like the claps? You can sing, too.

Play "Lavender's Blue" as in activity 3 above, while the children dance as Dancing Bear. Encourage them to move like the swing and the clap, in a dotted half-note (𝅗𝅥.) rhythm, slowly and easily.

Have one child stand at the side and turn the music box handle.

7

Put 𝅘𝅥 and 𝅘𝅥 𝅘𝅥𝅮 on the chalkboard.

On a shelf in the shop are the toys that walk. Everybody can be a high-stepping horse going all around the circle.

If needed, use two chairs to define a circle.

Have the children initiate the movement. Then, perhaps after once around the circle, play the piano or another pitched instrument as they continue to step.

Play "High-Stepping Horses" from Lesson 4. Play it about twice through.

Ask the children to point to the walking note on the board. Also ask if anyone recognized the song. Most children will.

8 There's another shelf in the shop that has toys that gallop. There's an especially beautiful brown galloping pony there.

Have the children initiate the galloping pony movement. Then play "I'm Riding on My Pony" from Lesson 10.

Ask the children to point to the galloping note on the board. Also ask if anyone recognized the song. Most children will.

Story Time

Read the story aloud. Then read it aloud again as the individual parts are carried out in movement and song by the children. One child or any number of children can take an individual part.

Characters
Elves
High-Stepping Horses
Galloping Ponies
Dancing Bear

(Walking note cards)
(Galloping note cards)

Every toy you could think of was to be found in Mr. Jones's Toy Shop. There were trains, toy soldiers, high-stepping horses, galloping ponies, even a dancing bear with its own music box.

But everything was so helter-skelter that Mr. Jones could never find what a customer wanted.

One night, when all was still, the elf box opened. The biggest of the elves stepped out. He said to everyone, "If we have signs, Mr. Jones can find us easily." He took out a pile of cards. "Let's see. Who goes with a walking note?"

"We do," said the High-Stepping Horses. They each took a walking note card from the Elf. Then they stepped around in perfect time.

(The Horses take cards and step around.)

Play on the piano or another pitched instrument:

But who was *this* coming out? Dancing Bear!

(Dancing Bear comes out.)

"No, no," everyone said. "Not yet, Dancing Bear." Dancing Bear went back to a corner.

(Dancing Bear goes back.)

The Elf took out the galloping cards. "Now," he said, "the gallopers." All the Ponies came out, took cards, and went galloping around the room.

(The Ponies take cards and gallop.)

Oh, my, here was Dancing Bear *again*!

(Dancing Bear comes out.)

"No, no," everyone said. "Not yet, Dancing Bear."
Dancing Bear went back to a corner.

(Dancing Bear goes back.)

"Let's sing Dancing Bear's music so he'll know it," said
the stuffed giraffe. So everyone sang Dancing Bear's music.
The sound was slow and sweet. The card was a slow note with
a dot.

(Everyone sings "Lavender's Blue.")

Play on the piano or
other pitched
instrument as all sing:

Then one of the elves turned the music box handle so that
everyone could dance to Dancing Bear's music. Of course,
Dancing Bear held his card and danced, too.

Play as above as
everyone sings and
dances.

(All sing and dance, moving on the slow note— ♩. —marked x
on the song.)

The next day, Mr. Jones could find any toy a customer
wanted. It was the best toy shop in town.

The End

Lesson 35

Hot Cross Buns

Moderato

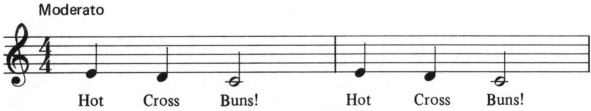

Hot   Cross   Buns!   Hot   Cross   Buns!

One   a   pen - ny,   Two   a   pen - ny,   Hot   Cross   Buns!

179

Lesson 35
HOT CROSS BUNS

1   It's Easter time and the Easter Bunny is out looking for eggs to put in his basket. He's in the country. He is glad to see the sheep in the fields and the birds flying about and the flowers growing everywhere. Maybe you should help the Easter Bunny.

Everyone can go out and look for eggs. When you find one, come and put it in this basket.

(Imaginary play.) Have a basket into which the "eggs" are placed, somewhere in the room. All the children can go about the room and find an "egg" to put in the basket.

2   Good. I think the Easter Bunny will come for the eggs soon. Someone else comes at Easter time. It's the man who sells hot cross buns. He has a song that he sings everywhere he goes. Listen—

Sing the song and teach it to the children.

3   Put the rhythms of the song on the board in lines like this:

This song is like a sandwich with two pieces of bread on top.

Point to the notes as you show:

{ Hot cross buns   { Two slices of bread
{ Hot cross buns   {

One a penny, two a penny—Filling

Hot cross buns—One slice of bread

Give individual children a turn to go to the board and point to the notes that say "hot cross buns" (two times on the top and once on the bottom), as they sing the words.

4   **Now who will come and point to the notes that say "One a penny, two a penny?"**

Give individual children a turn to go to the board and point to the notes for "One a penny, two a penny" as they sing.

Recognition of the line is sufficient. Accuracy in pointing to each eighth note is not essential.

5 Suppose we were selling Easter eggs with the same kind of sandwich shape to our song. Let's make a drawing on the chalkboard as we go along.

Have the children take turns to add a line to the drawing until it is completed.

Easter eggs

Easter eggs

One a penny, two a penny

Easter eggs

6 Good. Now let's sing our new words with the melody we know.

Play as for activity 2 above, as the children sing the song with the words for "Easter eggs."

7 How about selling lollipops the same way? Listen carefully and call out the last line.

Say: Lollipops
Lollipops
One a penny, two a penny
Children call: Lollipops

8 Now everyone can call out this last line:

Say: Choc'late pie
Choc'late pie
One a penny, two a penny,
Children call: Choc'late pie

9

Have the children seated or standing where they can see the keyboard.

Our melody for "Hot Cross Buns" starts on the top side of these two black notes and comes straight down, like this:

(Show.) Play with your middle finger, one note at a time, as you sing:

Sing: Hot Cross Buns
Play: E   D   C

Give several children a turn to sing and play the same.

10 If I stay on the same note and go back the way I came, I can play "One a penny, two a penny" like this—

(Show.) Play, again with your middle finger, one note at a time as you sing:

Sing: One a penny, two a penny
Play C C C   D D D

Give several children turns to sing and play the same.

11 Good. Now let's do our song this way—

(Show.) Sing and play "Hot Cross Buns":

E   D   C
Hot cross buns
E   D   C

Sing only: One a penny, two a penny
Sing and play: Hot cross buns

E   D   C

12   Have two temple blocks, one tambourine, and a third temple block placed in a row. Select one player for each instrument.

Each player will play his or her instrument with one line of our "Hot Cross Buns" song as we sing. Which player should start first if all the instruments play in a row?

Some children will see that the first of the two temple blocks must start first.

Play as for activity 2 as all the children sing "Hot Cross Buns." The instruments play as everyone sings and you play.

1st temple block: ♩ ♩ ♩

2nd temple block: ♩ ♩ ♩

Tambourine: shakes, without a specified rhythm

3rd temple block: ♩ ♩ ♩

Give other children a turn to play the instruments as you play and the rest of the children sing.

13 Would you like to sing your own melody for "Hot Cross Buns" or maybe for "Easter Eggs" or "Lollipops"? The instruments can play with you, too.

Suggest the possibility of singing the same melody for the repeated "Easter Eggs:"

Easter eggs   (any pitches)
Easter eggs   (same as above)
One a penny, two a penny   (different)
Easter eggs   (like one and two)

If desirable, you can play the drum with the temple blocks.
Give several children a turn to improvise their own melodies.

14   Place finger cymbals on a table.

That was fine. Everyone can skip now. Maybe we'll see the Easter Bunny on the way. If you would rather play the finger cymbals, take a pair and come and stand together here.

Have the children who choose to play the finger cymbals stand together. Play Record 41-6089 S7B3 (Piano No. 13).

Story Time

Read the story aloud. Then read it aloud again as the individual parts are carried out in movement and song by the children.

Characters
The Muffin Man
Benjy
Amy
Joshua
The Townspeople

Play on the piano or another pitched instrument as the Muffin Man sings and pushes his cart:

Here was the man with the special buns for Easter and springtime. As he pushed his cart he sang.

(The Muffin Man pushes his cart and sings.)

Moderato

Hot Cross Buns, | Hot Cross Buns, | One a pen-ny, Two a pen-ny, | Hot Cross Buns.

How glad we were to see him! Everybody bought a bun. Then Benjy said, "I wish I had a cart. I would sell lollipops." And he sang, with the "Hot Cross Buns" melody:

Play as above as Benjy sings with "Lollipops."

**"Lollipops,
  Lollipops,
  One a penny, two a penny,
  Lollipops."**

(Benjy sings.)

Amy spoke up. "I would like to sell Easter eggs." She sang, with the same melody, too:

Play as above as Amy sings with "Easter Eggs."

**"Easter eggs,
  Easter eggs,
  One a penny, two a penny,
  Easter eggs."**

(Amy sings.)

"I bet people would buy choc'late pie," said Joshua. "How does this sound?" And he played on the piano (or xylophone) as he sang:

(Joshua plays and sings.)

**"Choc'late pie   (E-D-C)
  Choc'late pie   (E-D-C)
  One a penny, two a penny** *(Singing only)*
  Choc'late pie"   (E-D-C)

"That's great," said everybody. Then they all bought another bun and sang "Hot Cross Buns" with the hot cross bun man.

Play as all sing.

(All buy a bun and sing the song as above.)

The End

One-Two

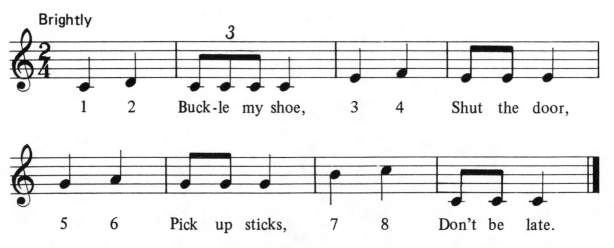

Brightly

1 2 Buck-le my shoe, 3 4 Shut the door,

5 6 Pick up sticks, 7 8 Don't be late.

Lesson 36
ONE—TWO

1

You will need number cards about 8″ × 8″ numbered 1 through 8.

Once a family of ponies had to cross over a shaky bridge. The eldest said, "If we go one at a time, the bridge won't fall down." So that is what they did. You can show us how they went. The drum will tell you if you should gallop across, or step high, or maybe even trot.

Give each of eight children a number card and have them wait to "cross the bridge" on one side of the room. (Two chairs placed on opposite sides of the room can mark the bridge.)

Play for each "pony" to go across the bridge, in the numbered order. Play the drum differently for each one, in a gallop, fast, or slow:

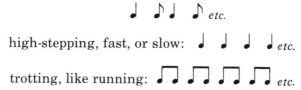

high-stepping, fast, or slow:

trotting, like running:

On the other side of the bridge, have the first group give their cards to eight other children, who now come across one by one as you play the drum. Again, play the drum differently for each one.

2

Draw the scale on the chalkboard (going up only) with numbers underneath.

Here are the same numbers going up on our music ladder. We need someone to go to the board and point to the numbers while we sing.

Give children a turn to go to the chalkboard and point as all the children sing the numbers, raising one arm as they sing.

Play the drum as the children all sing and one child points to the number. Vary the tempo very slightly as you repeat the scale several times.

Example: Play for one scale in a moderate tempo, a second scale in a little faster than moderate tempo, and a third scale a little slower than moderate tempo.

3   **This is a song with numbers that we can use for lots of games. Listen—**

Sing the song and teach it to the children.

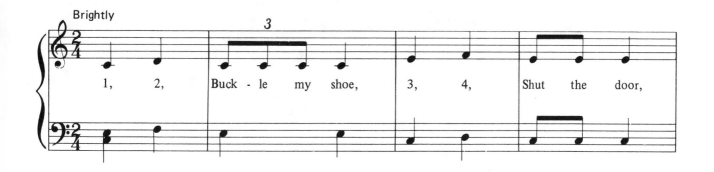

5, 6,   Pick   up   sticks,   7,   8,   Don't   be   late.

4   Good. Now we'll have a game.

> Have the children form two lines facing each other. Each line is a team. The first one in line A says, "One, two, buckle my shoe," and then the first one in line B says, "Three, four, shut the door," and so on, continuing to the end of the lines.
>
> *Example:*
>
> | *First line* | *Second line* |
> |---|---|
> | 1, 2 Buckle my shoe — — — — = = | 3, 4 Shut the door |
> | 5, 6, Pick up sticks =‑‑ ‑ — — = | 7, 8, Don't be late |
> | 1, 2, Buckle my shoe =‑‑ — — — | 3, 4, Shut the door |
>
> Play the drum on the beat as everyone speaks. Whoever misses the next number or does not come in on time is "out."
>
> Gradually increase the speed of your drum beat to make it a game. The team that has the least out is the winner.

5

> You will need four cards about 8″ × 8″ with the following numbers and pictures drawn on each. Place them on a flat surface, face up.

(Benjy), will you pick up the card that says "1, 2, Buckle my shoe"?

> Give the children turns to pick up the card asked for (any one of the four cards).

6   "One *two*" rhymes with "*shoe.*" What could I say instead of "buckle my shoe"? Maybe "one *two*, What can I *do*?" or "One, *two*, Have some *stew*."

> Have the children make up their own substitutions for each set of numbers. Any sensible or nonsense words are good, if they go along with the rhythm of the chant. You might encourage words or syllables that rhyme.
>
> *Examples:*   3, 4, Apple core
>   or   3, 4, Give me more
>
>   5, 6, Make a mix
>   or   5, 6, I do tricks
>
>   7, 8, Pick a plate
>   or   7, 8, Eat a date

7   **(Amy), you can play your own chant on the drum. Say the words as you play.**

Give children a turn to play their own words on the drum. Have them play the drum rhythm with the words.

Example: Speaking 7, 8, Pick a plate

Drum—   ♪   ♪   ♫   ♪

8   Place a chair in each of the four corners of the room, leaving enough space around each chair for passage. Number the corners 1-2, 3-4, 5-6, 7-8. Try to see that the children know clearly the numbers of the different corners.

Each corner has numbers like the ones in our song. When I call out a number, skip in that corner.

Play Record 41-6088 S6B5 (Piano No. 4).

188

Story Time

Read the story aloud. Then read it aloud again as the individual parts are carried out in movement and song by the children. One or any number of children can take an individual part.

Characters
All the children in the
  classroom
Amy
Benjy
Joshua
Janie

The four cards of the
chant, with pictures

Everyone was gathered in the corner of the room. A big sign said "Games."

"Gosh, look at this one," called Amy as she pushed around a big jigsaw puzzle. "How do you think this gets put together?"

She spread the pieces on the floor. There were four cards. Everyone could see that the game was to put the cards in the right order.

Joshua picked up a card. He held it up. He said, "3, 4, Pick up sticks."

(Joshua picks up a card.)

Janie picked up a card. She held it up, too, as she said, "7, 8, Don't be late."

(Janie picks up a card.)

Benjy picked up a card. He held it up. He said, "1, 2, Buckle my shoe."

(Benjy picks up a card.)

Amy picked up the last card. She held it up and said, "5, 6, Pick up sticks."

(Amy picks up the last card.)

Then Amy put everyone with a card in a line, so the cards read like this: 1-2, 3-4, 7-8.

(Amy puts everyone in a line.)

"That looks pretty good," said Joshua, "but how come Amy's card is left over?"

"It comes after '3, 4, Shut the door,'" shouted Janie. "Right," said everyone, and then Amy stood in her place in the line.

(Amy stands in her place in the line.)

Play the drum as
everyone chants.

Now the whole class chanted:

  1, 2, Buckle my shoe
  3, 4, Shut the door
  5, 6, Pick up sticks
  7, 8, Don't be late

(The class chants.)

That was a good game!

The End

Lesson 37

Hot or Cold

Moderato

Pease por - ridge hot, pease por - ridge cold,
Some like it hot, some like it cold,

Pease por - ridge in the pot, nine days old.
Some like it in the pot, nine days old.

Lesson 37
HOT OR COLD

1   Let's skip together. When I play strongly skip the same way, and when I play softly skip very softly.

Have the children skip as you play, first strongly and then very softly. (Their skips will be high when strong and close to the floor when very soft.

Play on the piano or another pitched instrument (or on the drum). Repeat either part ad lib.

2   The children are seated.

Good. I think some of you know this chant. Everybody swing with me and say it, too, if you know it.

Swing from side to side in your seat, as you say:

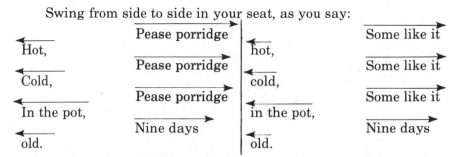

Repeat this several times, swinging with the children.

3   Now we'll do the chant in different ways.

Have the children take partners and stand facing each other. Ask them to take hands and to swing from side to side as they say the chant.

(Amy) and (Jane), will you show us how you would say the chant very slowly while you swing your arms together?

(Swing as in activity 2 above.)
Have two children initiate the movement in a very slow tempo as they say the chant. (One verse is sufficient.) Then all join in.
Play the rhythm of the chant on the drum as everyone says the chant.
The swing is long because of the slow tempo.

P-e-a-s-e P-o-r-r-i-d-g-e

H-o-t

4   (Benjy) and (Josh), show us how you would swing and speak fast.

Have two children initiate the swing in a fast tempo while saying the chant in the same fast tempo. (One verse is sufficient.) Then all join in, swinging their arms with their partners and saying the chant. Do two verses.
Play the drum with the rhythm of the chant.
The swing is short because of the fast tempo.

Pease Porridge

Hot

Either activity 3 or activity 4 may be repeated as desired.

5   Some people like to say it very strongly. (Amy), will you step and say the chant very strongly? Then everybody will join in.

Have one child begin stepping as he or she says the chant very strongly. Then all the other children join in, stepping on the beat.
Play the rhythm of the chant on the drum and say the chant with the children, strongly.
The step is a large one because of the energy in loud dynamics.

Example:

(Step)
PEASE PORRIDGE

(Step)
HOT,

(Step)
PEASE PORRIDGE

(Step)
COLD,   etc.

6   Some people like to say the chant very softly. (Benjy), will you step and say the chant very softly? Then everybody will join in.

Have one child begin stepping on the beat as he or she says the chant very softly. Then all the other children join in.
Play the rhythm of the chant on the drum and say the chant with the children, very softly.

The step is a very small one because of the lesser energy in soft dynamics.

Example:
                              (Step)
          (Step)   Pease porridge
          hot,   *(Step)*
          (Step)   Pease porridge
          cold,

7   Good.

Draw two lines like these on the chalkboard:

One of these lines is for the swing when I say our chant slowly. The other line is for when I say the chant fast. (Amy), will you go to the board and draw the rest of the lines while you say the chant slowly?

Have one child go to the board and say the chant slowly while making the additional long lines.

Example:

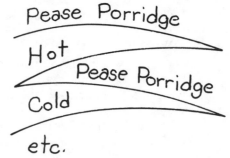

One child can do one verse and another child can do the second verse in the same slow tempo.

Give another child a turn to go to the board and say the chant fast, while making the short lines.

Example:

One child can do one verse and another child can do the second verse in the same fast tempo.

8   We can use the same lines for loud and soft. But I'll make the short lines even lighter and the long line very dark because I draw it so strongly.

(Show.) Draw a long line, very strongly: ▬▬▬▬▬▬

and a short line, very lightly: ─────

Give individual children a turn to go to the board and say a part of the chant, either strongly or softly as they draw the lines.

9   Some people like to sing about the porridge like this—

Sing the song and teach it to the children.

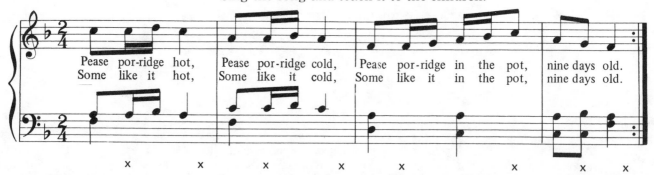

Pease por-ridge hot,   Pease por-ridge cold,   Pease por-ridge in the pot,   nine days old.
Some like it hot,   Some like it cold,   Some like it in the pot,   nine days old.

10 This song is especially good with a beat that you might hear in music on the TV. Listen—

Clap for the children as you swing and sing. Then all do the same. (The clap is syncopated, marked *x* in the song.)

Pease porridge
(Clap)

Hot,
(Clap)

Pease porridge
(Clap)

Cold,
(Clap)

Pease porridge
(Clap)

in the pot,
(Clap)

Nine days
(Clap)

Old,
(Clap)

11 It's time to stir the porridge. First we'll do it together.

> Have all the children sit on the floor, feet crossed in front. All say the chant as they "stir the pot," making a circle in time with the beat.
>
> *Example:*

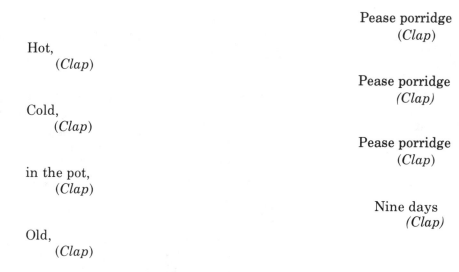

Pease porridge hot,

12 Good. Now everyone can skip with the drum. When you hear the rhythm of "Pease porridge hot," sit down right away on the floor and stir your porridge. Be sure to make a big circle if I play slowly or strongly and a small circle if I play fast or softly.

> Play the skipping rhythm in a moderate speed on the drum. (The children skip with you.) Alternate the skipping rhythm with the rhythm of "Pease porridge hot," one verse played fast or slow, strong or soft.
>
> When the children hear the rhythm of the chant, they sit on the floor and "stir the pot" in the same speed or dynamics as your drum beats.
>
> *Example:* You play on the drum
> while the children skip. ♩ ♪♩ ♪♩ ♪ *etc.*
>
> You play

> very slowly. The children sit on the floor and stir the pot very
> slowly in a big circle.
>
> You play the skipping rhythm on the drum again (♩ ♪♩ ♪ *etc.*)
> while the children skip.
>
> Then you play

> very fast, as the children sit on the floor and stir the pot very fast
> with a small circle.
>
> Alternate the skipping rhythm also with the chant rhythm played very
> softly and very strongly.

Story Time

Characters
The King
The First Cook
The Second Cook
The Third Cook
The Fourth Cook
The King's Countrymen

Play the drum fast in the rhythm of the verse as the First Cook chants:

Play the drum in the rhythm of the verse, very slowly, as the Second Cook chants:

Play the drum loudly in the rhythm of the verse as the Third Cook chants:

Play the drum in the rhythm of the verse very softly as the Fourth Cook chants:

Read the story aloud. Then read it aloud again as the individual parts are carried out in movement and song by the children.

Once upon a time there was a King who liked his pease porridge to be cooked just right. So his messengers went everywhere in the land to bring the best cooks to the palace. Now the King and all his people were here. The cooks were here, too, each one hoping that he was the best.

How fast the first cook stirred! What little circles his spoon made!

(The first cook stirs as he chants.)

Pease porridge hot,
Pease porridge cold,
Pease porridge in the pot,
Nine days old.

The King tested the porridge.

(The King tastes the porridge.)

"Ugh," he said. "That's lumpy."
The second cook stirred the pot very slowly. His spoon went out to the very edge of the pot.

(The second cook stirs as he chants.)

P-e-a-s-e p-o-r-r-i-d-g-e h-o-t
P-e-a-s-e p-o-r-r-i-d-g-e c-o-l-d
P-e-a-s-e p-o-r-r-i-d-g-e i-n t-h-e p-o-t,
N-i-n-e d-a-y-s o-l-d.

(The King tastes the porridge.)

"Ugh," said the King. "That's too smooth. Like paste."
Now the third cook tried. He hoped to show how strongly he could stir, and he said the words very loudly as he stirred with great circles.

(The third cook stirs as he chants.)

PEASE PORRIDGE HOT,
PEASE PORRIDGE COLD,
PEASE PORRIDGE IN THE POT,
NINE DAYS OLD.

But most of the porridge splashed out, and there was hardly any left for the King to taste.
The last cook whispered as he made tiny circles.

(The last cook whispers as he stirs.)

pease porridge hot,
pease porridge cold,
pease porridge in the pot,
nine days old.

"Oh, dear," said the King. "This is hardly cooked at all."
So he made himself a bowl of porridge, and it was just right!
Then he gave a great porridge feast for all his people, and everyone sang "Pease porridge Hot" and clapped with the special beat.

Play the piano or other
pitched instrument as
all sing and clap
(marked *x* in song):

The End

Special Piano Arrangements

1 *Flying Birds*

Anderson

2 Galloping Horses

Anderson

3 Running Horses

Anderson

4 *Skipping Theme*

Anderson

5 *Wheelbarrow Motive*

Anderson

6 *Happy and Light of Heart*

Balfe

7 *Valsette*

Borowski

8 La Bergeronette Burgmuller

9 Run, Run Concone

10 *Gigue*

Corelli

11 *Valse Gracieuse*

Dvorak

12 *Ballet*

Gluck

13 *Sicilienne*

Gluck

14 *Postillion*

Godard

15 *Mirror Dance*

Gounod

16 *March*

Gurlitt

17 *Running Game*

Gurlitt

18 *Scherzo*

Gurlitt

19 *March*

Hollaender

20 *Elfenspiel*

Kjerulf

21 *Skating*

Kullak

22 *Tarantelle*

Mendelssohn

23 *Sparks*

Moskowski

24 *Dwarfs*

Poldini

25 *Gnomes*

Reinhold

26 *Silhouette*

Reinhold

27 *Jaglied*

Schumann

28 *Papillons*

Schumann

29 Soldier's March Schumann

Energetic

f

f

30 The Doll's Funeral Tschaikowsky

Slowly

pp

Fine

Da Capo al Fine

31 *March of the Tin Soldiers*

Tschaikowsky

32 *March "Nutcracker"*

Tschaikowsky

33 *Song of the Shepherdess*

Weber

34 Come Lasses and Lads

35 John Peel

36 Oats, Peas, Beans

37 The Big Gray Cat